DATE DUE

Tony Musante, Frances Conroy, Baxter Harris, Celia Weston, Maureen Anderman and Irene Worth in a scene from the New York production of "The Lady From Dubuque." Setting designed by Rouben Ter-Arutunian.

EDWARD ALBEE'S
THE LADY
FROM
DUBUQUE

★

★

DRAMATISTS
PLAY SERVICE
INC.

THE LADY FROM DUBUQUE
Copyright © 1980, Edward Albee
Copyright © 1977, 1979, Edward Albee
as an unpublished dramatic composition

All Rights Reserved

FOR

STEFANI HUNZINGER

—FROM THE BEGINNING

PLAYS BY

EDWARD ALBEE

(Dates of Composition)

ADAPTATIONS

THE LADY FROM DUBUQUE
FIRST PERFORMANCE
January 31, 1980, The Morosco Theater, New York City

LUCINDA	Celia Weston
SAM	Tony Musante
JO	Frances Conroy
FRED	Baxter Harris
EDGAR	David Leary
CAROL	Maureen Anderman
OSCAR	Earle Hyman
ELIZABETH	Irene Worth

Directed by Alan Schneider

Setting	Rouben Ter-Arutunian
Costumes	John Falabella
Lighting	Richard Nelson
Stage Manager	Julia Gillett

CHARACTERS

The characters in order of speaking are:

SAM—a good looking, thinnish man; 40

JO—a frail, lovely, dark-haired girl; early 30's

FRED—a blond ex-athlete going to fat; 40

LUCINDA—your average blonde housewife; 35

EDGAR—balding perhaps; average; 40

CAROL—brunette; ripe; 30

OSCAR—an elegant, thin black man; 50 or so

ELIZABETH—a stylish, elegant, handsome woman; splendid for whatever her age.

SET

A living room with stairs to the second floor and a balcony; a bay window; an all-purpose entrance hall.

I see the environment as uncluttered, perhaps with a Bauhaus feeling. No decorator has been at work; what we see is the taste of the occupants. I think the predominant color should be light grey.

PERFORMANCE NOTE

With some regularity throughout this play the characters address the audience—usually in brief asides, but occasionally at greater length. This is done without self-consciousness, quite openly, and without interrupting the flow of the play. In other words, the characters are aware of the presence of the audience, and since the audience has always been there, the characters are not upset by it, even though there are times they wish it would go away.

It is of utmost importance that the actors make it clear that it is not they, but the characters, who are aware of the presence of the audience.

Speeches to the audience (asides, etc.) are clearly marked, as is their termination.

EDWARD ALBEE

Edward Albee was born March 12, 1928, and began writing plays thirty years later. His plays are, in order of composition: *The Zoo Story; The Death of Bessie Smith; The Sandbox; The American Dream; Who's Afraid of Virginia Woolf?; The Ballad of the Sad Cafe* (adapted from Carson McCuller's novella); *Tiny Alice; Malcolm* (adapted from James Purdy's novel); *A Delicate Balance; Everything in the Garden* (adapted from a play by Giles Cooper); *Box and Quotations from Chairman Mao Tse-Tung; All Over; Seascape; Listening; Counting the Ways* and *The Lady From Dubuque.*

The Lady From Dubuque

ACT ONE

Sam, Jo, Fred, Carol, Edgar, and Lucinda Onstage. Edgar Center, his back to the audience; Fred at the bar; Sam at the window seat; the others seated or sprawled. It is midnight; they are tired and they have been drinking a little.

The group applauds Edgar as the curtain rises; he bows to them, exaggerated, mocking. They are playing Twenty Questions, and Edgar has finished his turn.

LUCINDA. Good for Edgar! Good for you, Edgar!

SAM. (*Rises, moves Center, as Edgar moves to sit.*) O.K., now; my turn. (*As the others mumble to each other.*) All right, now; silence! It's my turn! Who am I?

JO. Well, if you don't know who you are, I don't see . . .

FRED. Who's talking?

SAM. C'mon, Fred!

FRED. Who's *talking!?*

EDGAR. O.K., give the man some silence.

JO. The man asked for silence; give it to him.

SAM. From the wives, too?

JO. (*Deep voice.*) From the wives, too.

FRED. Who's *talking?*

LUCINDA. You are, for one, Fred.

CAROL. Leave Fred alone.

SAM. From the wives? Please? The girl friends and the wives?

JO. The man asked for silence; give it to him; he doesn't know who he is.

FRED. (*Clapping.*) O.K.! O.K.! Let's have a little silence for the man.

SAM. Come on, gang; you've all had a turn, and now it's mine.

FRED. Carol didn't have a turn. Why is it your turn?

SAM. Carol didn't *want* a turn. Besides, it's my house, and you're drinking my liquor, and it's my turn.

FRED. (*Shrugs; sits.*) You can't argue with logic.

EDGAR. (*To create order.*) O.K. one more time; Sam's turn; Sam goes.

LUCINDA. Remember! Edgar's winning! You all took twelve to get Edgar.

FRED. (*Bored.*) Good old Edgar.

EDGAR. (*Hand in champ pose, but weary.*) Yea for me.

SAM. Let me have silence; *please!* Who *am* I?

JO. The man asked for silence; give it to him. Poor man: he doesn't know who he is.

LUCINDA. Let there be silence! (*There is silence.*)

SAM. Well; at last! Thank you! Twenty questions . . . who *am* I?

JO. (*Leans forward; to the audience.*) Don't you just hate party games? Don't you just hate them? (*Turns her attention back.*)

SAM. (*To Jo, commenting on her involving the audience.*) Come on! Don't do that! (*To the others.*) Twenty questions! Who *am* I?

FRED. (*Bored.*) Your name is *Sam;* this is your *house* . . .

CAROL. Stop it, Fred; I don't want any help.

FRED. I'm not giving you any!

CAROL. So *you* say.

FRED. Jesus!

SAM. Who am I! Come on! Who am I!?

JO. (*Rote.*) Your name is Sam; this is your house; they're drinking your liquor . . .

SAM. Awwww, Jo . . .

JO. Your name is Sam, and this is your house, and I am your wife, and I am dying . . .

SAM. (*Private.*) Don't, Jo. (*To the others.*) Come on, gang. Who am I?

EDGAR. (*Sighs.*) O.K. one more time.

LUCINDA. Let's play!

JO. (*Shrugs.*) O.K. let's play. (*To the audience.*) What can you do? He's a nice man. (*Her attention back to the others.*)

EDGAR. *Are* you a man?

SAM. No.

JO. Coulda fooled *me.*

CAROL. (*To Fred.*) Then he's a woman.

FRED. Of course he's a woman! What the fuck do you think he is!?

CAROL. (*Getting angry.*) He could be a dog, or a horse, or something!

FRED. A horse!? What do you mean, a horse? Nobody's ever been a horse! You're always embarrassing me!

CAROL. I'm trying to learn the game! You want me to fit in, don't you? Well? Besides, what's embarrassing about a horse?

JO. (*As if the question were to be answered.*) What's embarrassing about a horse? Well, lets see . . . (*To the audience.*) They're certainly no brighter than you'd want them to be.

SAM. Aw, come on! Hunh? Jo? Please? (*Jo shrugs, turns her attention back in.*)

EDGAR. (*Bored.*) Play the game; play the game.

CAROL. (*To Sam, very unsure of herself.*) You a horse, or something?

SAM. (*Smiles.*) Nope; nothing like that.

JO. (*To the guests.*) *And* . . . they're said to bear grudges, but with their tiny brains, I wonder.

LUCINDA. (*An announcement.*) Neither a man nor a horse. That's two.

CAROL. (*To Fred; not pleasant.*) So he's a woman, hunh?

FRED. Ask him!

CAROL. What!? Ask him if he's a woman? I just asked him if he was a horse.

FRED. (*Enjoying it finally.*) Yeah; ask him; ask him if he's a woman.

CAROL. (*Tiny pause.*) You a woman?

SAM. (*Smiles.*) No, I'm not a woman; that's three.

CAROL. (*To Fred; enraged with embarrassment.*) You see!?

FRED. Whadda you mean you're not a woman!? You're not a man, you gotta be a woman! What are you: one of those sex changes, or something?

SAM. (*Laughs.*) No, I am not one of *those.* That's four down.

EDGAR. Hey, hey, wait! Are you more than one person?

SAM. (*Pleased.*) Right!

FRED. Ah, for Christ's . . .

EDGAR. How many people are you? You two people?

SAM. Right; two people; that's six questions.

EDGAR. He's two people, gang. Uh . . . men?

SAM. Right.

LUCINDA. Living!

SAM. Wrong; that's eight.

EDGAR. O.K. Two dead people; both men.

FRED. Probably a couple of queers! Famous queers!

JO. You *would* think of that, Fred.

EDGAR. O.K. Let's see . . . Marx and Engels.

LUCINDA. (*A loud whisper.*) Were they queer?

EDGAR. Of course not!

CAROL. (*To Fred.*) Marx and who?

FRED. Engels! Marx and Engels!

JO. (*To Carol; helpful.*) The Kaufman and Hart of their day.

SAM. (*Rueful laugh.*) Oh ho, you just wait!

LUCINDA. (*Bright.*) Gilbert and Sullivan, Rimbaud and Verlaine
. . .

CAROL. (*General.*) Who *are* these people!?

JO. They're foreign, Carol.

SAM. That makes eleven.

JO. They're not foreign?

SAM. No! They're not who she said!

FRED. Lum and Abner, Abbott and Costello, Sacco and Vazetti,
uh . . .

SAM. Nope, nope, nope; fourteen.

EDGAR. Hey, you're not playing it right, guessing wild like that.
You gotta be scientific.

JO. Old people, Sam? Very old people? (*To the audience.*) I know
who it is. (*Her attention back to the group.*)

CAROL. They're dead!

FRED. (*Trying to remain pleasant.*) She means a long time ago,
Carol.

CAROL. (*Not convinced.*) Oh.

SAM. (*Still enthusiastic.*) Yes, old people; long time ago; long, long
time ago.

JO. Were they brothers, Sam? (*To the audience.*) I know who it *is*.
(*Her attention back to the group.*)

SAM. Were they . . . ? (*He realizes Jo knows the answer.*) Aw, that's
not fair, Jo.

LUCINDA. (*Happy.*) What's not fair!?

EDGAR. (*Brows knitted.*) Yeah. What's not fair?

SAM. Jo knows who it is; that's not fair.

FRED. (*The edge of anger.*) What do you mean it's not fair!? It's a
game, isn't it? She knows, she knows.

SAM. Wives shouldn't be allowed to play.

FRED. (*Stern.*) Wives play; girl friends play; husbands play; everybody plays. Who the fuck is it, Jo?

JO. (*Smiles.*) Brothers, Sam? A long time ago? And these brothers, by the faintest of possibilities did they happen to be suckled by a wolf, and did they happen to found the city of Rome?

SAM. (*Real down.*) Yes, yes. Fifteen, sixteen, something; I win.

LUCINDA. Oh, *what's* their name!? Remus and something.

EDGAR. (*Overly clear.*) Romulus and Remus.

CAROL. (*To Fred.*) I don't *know* any of these people!

JO. Don't worry, Carol; you wouldn't have liked them.

SAM. I win. Big deal. It's no fair—really. (*To the audience.*) Really; it's no fair. (*Back to the others.*)

EDGAR. Sore winner.

SAM. She knew who it was; she could figure it out! (*To the audience.*) She knew all along. (*Back to the others.*)

EDGAR. Awwwwwwwww!

CAROL. (*To Jo.*) How'd you know?

JO. Weeeeellll . . .

SAM. Aw, come on, Jo!

JO. (*To quiet Sam.*) No, I think it's nice, shows we . . . I think it's nice. (*To the others.*) Sam and I were in bed a couple of nights ago—talking and sort of lying around—and he was stroking me—which is about it, now; hey, gang?

EDGAR. (*Profound sadness.*) Aw, Jo.

JO. (*To the audience; a little rueful herself.*) Death's door, and all. *And* . . . he had one of my breasts, and he was sort of bouncing it around a little bit . . .

FRED. (*To Sam.*) You debbil!

JO. (*Still to the audience.*) . . . and he started nibbling, and then he started sucking . . .(*To Sam.*) . . . which breast was it, Sam?

SAM. (*Embarrassed, therefore cold.*) I don't recall: I was occupied. (*Refers to the audience.*) For God's sake, Jo!

JO. (*To Sam; kind.*) It's all right. (*To the audience.*) You don't mind if I talk about my breasts, do you? Humor the lady a little? (*To Sam.*) *They* don't mind. (*To the guests.*) Which breast *was* it—left, I think. And . . . he said—all of a sudden—he said he was Romulus, and I was the she-wolf, and I asked where his brother Remus was, and he told me not to be greedy . . .

SAM. O.K.! Big deal! (*A mocking chorus of "Awwwww, poor Sam; Aw, what's the matter, Sam?; he's embarrassed!" etc.*) O.K.! O.K.!

LUCINDA. (*"Isn't he too cute for words?"*) Aww . . .

SAM. (*To the audience.*) Now, if you want to know the real and true reason I wouldn't tell her where my brother Remus was . . .

13

JO. Was that you'd killed him! (*To the audience.*) He'd built the city—Rome—and he was standing around looking at the fortifications—very proud of himself—and Remus came up, took one look, and said, "Wow! Are those ever lousy fortifications." (*To Sam, now.*) And you killed him. Right on the spot.

LUCINDA. What an unpleasant thing to do!

FRED. (*Leans forward in his chair.*) Oh, *I* don't know; a man's proud of his fortifications.

JO. (*A trifle glum.*) Anyhow, that's how it was. Sam wins. I guess it, and Sam wins.

EDGAR. (*Not much enthusiasm.*) Anyhow, Sam wins; Sam's the champ. Game's over; hurray!

SAM. (*Playing Romulus; speculative.*) I was always jealous of Remus; I never knew why.

JO. What was it, did he hog the nipples? How many do wolves *have*, for God's sake.

SAM. Oh, there were enough . . . but he took my favorites.

FRED. (*Laughing.*) The four or five you liked the most.

SAM. Something like that.

JO. (*Glum.*) At least you had a *mother*.

SAM. (*Curiously annoyed.*) Oh, come on, Jo!

JO. (*Undaunted.*) WELL . . .

SAM. You've got a perfectly good mother!

JO. (*Clearly this is a private argument.*) Yeah? Where is she? Where the hell is she?

SAM. (*Spits it out.*) "In the hour of your need?"

JO. (*Hard.*) YEAH! IN THE HOUR OF MY GODDAMN NEED!!

EDGAR. Come on, Sam.

JO. Yeah? Big deal!

LUCINDA. (*Bright; maybe just to help.*) I've never met your mother!

JO. Big deal!

LUCINDA. (*Offended.*) Well. I'm sorry.

JO. (*Ugly mimicking.*) "Well. I'm sorry."

LUCINDA. I mean, I know she lives in New Jersey . . .

JO. Fuck New Jersey!

SAM. Jo . . .

LUCINDA. (*Grim.*) With her sister, is it?

JO. Fuck Jo's mother's sister!

SAM. Jo . . .

LUCINDA. (*Persisting.*) And you don't see her? Is that it?

EDGAR. Leave it alone, Lu.

LUCINDA. (*To Edgar; sotto voce.*) I was merely trying . . .

JO. Fuck merely trying.

SAM. C'mon, Jo.

JO. (*Perversely casual.*) O.K. O.K. by *me*.

SAM. (*To the audience.*) Jo's mother . . .

JO. (*Cheerful.*) Ah, fuck Jo's mother.

SAM. (*Still to the audience.*) The lady leaves something to be desired. She's tiny, thin as a rail, blue eyes—darting furtive blue eyes—

JO. Fuck furtive blue eyes.

SAM. (*Ibid.*) —pale hair, tinted pink, balding a little; you know; the way women do, when they do. We don't see her much. We don't like her; I don't like her.

LUCINDA. Still; a mother is a mother!

FRED. Jesus!

EDGAR. You just can't leave well enough alone, can you?

JO. "A mother is a mother." I like that!

SAM. (*To the others.*) Anyhow, game is over; *I* win: suckled by a wolf, fratricidal but victorious.

EDGAR. (*Claps his hands.*) Game's over, kids; game's over.

JO. (*Sarcastically enthusiastic.*) Yes, and wasn't it boring? Wasn't it all . . . empty, ultimately? Didn't we waste our time? (*To the audience; without emotion.*) Especially if you're dying, as I am.

SAM. (*So sad and weary.*) Come on, Jo. Please?

JO. (*Shrugs; to Sam, and generally to the guests.*) I merely wondered; it doesn't matter; I thought I'd ask; forget I said it.

SAM. Please, Jo?

FRED. (*Rises, empty glass in hand; moves toward the bar.*) Boring? I don't know. I thought it was like every other night around here; I thought it was fine.

SAM. (*To Jo.*) I mean, are you tired?

JO. (*Waves Sam off; to Fred.*) Is this the beginning of your hostility, Fred, or are you still pretending to be pleasant? I can never quite catch the moment when you turn. (*To the audience.*) Fred turns. (*Snaps her fingers.*) Just like that. (*Back to the group now.*)

CAROL. (*Generally.*) What did Fred do? (*To the audience.*) What did Fred do? (*Back to the group now.*)

FRED. (*Ponders, with a small smile.*) I'm still pretending to be pleasant, I think. Get anyone a drink?

CAROL. (*To no one in particular.*) Leave Fred alone; he's bad enough when he's awful.

FRED. I don't think I understand that, Carol. Who can I make a drink?

JO. (*Holding her empty glass out.*) Me.

SAM. (*Concerned.*) You all . . . you O.K.?

JO. (*Bravura.*) Sure.

FRED. (*Moves to Jo, takes her glass.*) A little night crap?

JO. A little what? A little night crap? Fred, you aren't vulgar, you're just plain dirt common.

FRED. You be careful now; I'm still pretending to be pleasant, but these social events are wearing on a man.

JO. Mmmmmmm; what a pity they're compulsory.

SAM. (*Guardedly pleased.*) Hey, come on; I'll think you two like each other.

FRED. (*Muses.*) Ooooh, I wouldn't worry, Sam; I like Jo a lot bettern'n Jo likes me. (*To Jo; twang.*) But ah'll make it up to ya, honey; you just see. (*Normal tone again.*) Lucinda? Is Edgar having another drink? (*Jo laughs.*)

LUCINDA. Well, ask *him*. Who do you think I *am*?

FRED. Carol? Edgar, what about it? Lucinda says ask *you*.

CAROL. None for me; it's hard enough to follow as it is.

EDGAR. Well . . . what does everyone think?

SAM. About what?

EDGAR. About having a *drink*. Should I have *another*?

SAM. (*A tiny pause.*) Most of us don't care, Edgar.

EDGAR. (*Curiously hurt.*) Oh. I see.

SAM. (*Mildly patronizing.*) I mean, it's the sort of thing a man's just got to decide for himself.

FRED. (*A drawl.*) Sam isn't being unfriendly, Edgar, just laying it on the line, as they say.

LUCINDA. You leave Edgar alone.

EDGAR. (*Grim.*) Gee, am I glad I asked.

SAM. (*Overly serious and solicitous.*) I think you ought to do what you want to, Edgar.

JO. (*A toast.*) Drink 'til you puke!

LUCINDA. (*Nervous distaste.*) Jo! That's not *like* you!

JO. I wasn't *talking* about *me;* I was talking about Edgar. If I were Edgar, I would drink 'til I puked. (*Small smile.*) No offense.

LUCINDA. (*An hysterical little laugh.*) Well! And none taken!

FRED. (*Friendly; an arm around Edgar.*) I'd think twice about having another drink if I were you, Edgar. My God, all the things that could happen? They coulda put poison in the ice cubes; it's three

16

blocks home . . . in the *dark;* the sky might fall? *And* . . . if Doomsday comes, mushroom Doomsday . . .

EDGAR. (*Quiet and as dignified as the situation allows.*) I think I will have a drink, Fred; I just think I will. (*He goes to the bar, pushing Fred aside.*)

SAM. (*Laughs, nicely.*) Oh, Edgar! Poor, sweet Edgar!

JO. (*Shy little girl imitation.*) The sky might fall? And Doomsday come? (*A long, hollow sound.*) Doooooooooooomsday!

EDGAR. (*A little put off.*) Don't you worry about me, Sam; I'm all right.

SAM. (*Looking at the bar; a small pause.*) Oh. Well. Well, in that case I'll get some more soda; we're out of soda. (*He begins to exit.*)

FRED. (*As Sam exits; broad.*) You're a good man, Sam!

JO. Dooooooomsday! (*To the audience.*) Doomsday. It follows Thursday . . . if you're lucky.

EDGAR. You all right, Jo?

FRED. (*Sitting, heavily.*) Good man, Sam. You have a good husband, Jo.

JO. (*Back to the others, now; to Fred; deep voice.*) Thanks, Fred. (*To Edgar; nice.*) Sure thing, Edgar; I'm O.K.

FRED. No, I mean it; he's O.K.

LUCINDA. (*Cheerful.*) Everybody likes Sam. Well, *I* like Sam, too.

FRED. (*None too pleasant.*) Hey, that's swell, Lucinda. (*To the audience.*) We *do* like Sam; Sam's really O.K. We like Sam a lot.

EDGAR. (*To the audience.*) Oh, we do; we *like* Sam.

JO. God! What are you planning to do—*knife* him, or something? (*Fred and Edgar turn their attention back to Jo.*)

FRED. (*Angry.*) We *like* him, for Christ's sake!

EDGAR. Come on, Jo!

JO. We *all* like Sam! Great! Big deal! (*Ruminative.*) We all like Sam, and that should make it Samsday. Samsday precedeth Doomsday: Samsday, Thurmsday, Doomsday. Isn't that how it goes, Fred?

FRED. (*Casual.*) *I* don't give a shit, Jo, *how* it goes; just *stop* it!

JO. O.K.

FRED. All I care about right now is my drink.

JO. (*A mock aside, to Carol.*) Fred really doesn't deserve Sam's friendship; Sam's too good for Fred; Sam knows it, but . . . well, you know.

FRED. (*Much too casual.*) Knock it off, Jo.

JO. (*To the audience.*) Sam's a real egalitarian; Sam pretends to

17

like everyone equally. (*Looks to Fred for his reaction; he gives her the finger.*)

CAROL. (*Looking at her nails.*) Sounds sort of indiscriminate to me.

JO. (*As Fred chuckles; briefly taken aback; to Carol.*) Well, yes, it *is* that. But Sam is a man of facets. Who *are* you, Carol?

CAROL. (*Stretches.*) Oooooooh, I'm a lady of parts; I got facets, too, you know.

FRED. She's a lady of parts.

CAROL. By which I mean I'm not all bimbo; I'm not your dumb brunette for nothing. I'm gonna go pee.

FRED. You, uh . . . you know where it is?

CAROL. (*Hand on hip; feigns puzzling it out.*) Well, let's see; it's either outdoors or inside, and since this is the sort of neighborhood's probably got zoning regulations I bet I'll find it somewhere here on the ground floor.

FRED. (*Sorry he brought it up.*) O.K. O.K.

CAROL. (*Relentless.*) And if I don't find it, I'll just squat on the rug. O.K.? O.K., lover?

FRED. O.K.! O.K.!

CAROL. (*To the audience, as she exits.*) God! These people!

JO. (*Looks after Carol.*) She's not bad; she's got a good mouth.

FRED. Carol's gonna marry me one day.

JO. (*In reaction to Fred's remark.*) Not a very good brain, maybe . . .

FRED. I'm a three-time winner; might as well make it four.

EDGAR. Have you asked her?

FRED. Hm?

EDGAR. Have you asked her to marry you!?

FRED. Have I *asked* her!? I ask her every night before we go to sleep; I ask her when we get up; I ask her when I'm in the saddle . . .

LUCINDA. (*Smiles at the memory.*) I made Edgar propose to me three times.

JO. (*After a slight pause.*) You take big chances, girl.

FRED. (*Intensely serious.*) Edgar, if I'd known that, I sure woulda been nicer to you all these years. I'll make it up to you, fella!

JO. (*Imitating.*) I'll make it up to you, fella! Big pal; big fella!

EDGAR. (*Weary.*) Lay off, Jo.

FRED. No, no, it's all right. (*Histrionic.*) Where else can you come in this cold world, week after week, as regular as patchwork, and be guaranteed ridicule and contempt? Where else, I ask you, in

18

this cold world? (*To the audience.*) There is nowhere else, in this cold world, where you can come, week after—

JO. (*Level.*) Oh, there must be lots of other places, Fred. *You* have friends; this can't be the only place.

EDGAR. Is the pain bad, Jo?

JO. (*Offhand.*) Pretty bad.

LUCINDA. (*A little dreamy.*) We love you, Fred; we all love each other.

JO. Speak for yourself, Lu.

FRED. (*Not to the audience.*) Name one; name one other place; name one other place where I can come and be *sure* of it, where I can *count* on it.

EDGAR. (*Bland.*) Well, you could come to *our* place, Fred; we got as much ridicule and contempt as the next house.

LUCINDA. (*Snapped out of her revery.*) We have not! (*To the audience.*) That is not true! (*To Edgar.*) Really, Edgar!

EDGAR. (*Dogmatic.*) Well, we *should.* If you are managing the house as you're supposed to, *if* you are keeping the larder full, then we should have just as much ridicule and contempt as the next . . .

FRED. (*Ruminative.*) *I* used to have *lots* of it—*closets* full; open a cupboard, and the ridicule and contempt'd just . . . fall out all over the place! I don't know what happened.

JO. (*Soothing.*) Well, maybe when you and Carol get married everything'll get back to normal.

FRED. (*Overly concerned.*) Gee; I sure hope so. (*A rumpus Offstage; the sound of Carol and Sam arguing. Carol catapults Onstage, followed by Sam with his soda bottles.*)

CAROL. (*At Sam.*) Just keep your fucking hands off me, that's all!!

SAM. Will you shut up!? Will you just—

CAROL. Goddamn creep! Goddamn son of a bitch! Jesus, you can't even go take a leak around here!

SAM. I said, shut up about it!

CAROL. Just keep your fucking hands off me!

FRED. (*Realizing what is happening.*) Hey hey hey hey!

CAROL. (*To Jo; quivering.*) You better put locks on your bathroom doors, lady, or handcuffs on this one!

FRED. Hey! What the hell *is* this!?

LUCINDA. (*Thrilled.*) What's going on!? What's going on!?

EDGAR. What *is* this?

19

SAM. (*Making weapons out of the soda bottles.*) Will you just shut up about it!?

CAROL. You dirty, dirty old man!

FRED. (*Getting to his feet; belligerent.*) O.K. now, just what the fuck's going—

CAROL. (*A sudden imitation of a violated maiden; falsetto.*) Fred? Would you take me home, please? I've been vastly insulted!

FRED. (*Ready for battle now.*) You're fuckin-A right I will! Jesus Christ, Sam! (*But Carol and Sam have dissolved into laughter, are hanging on to each other for support.*)

SAM. Oh, boy; oh, boy!

CAROL. Christ! Oh, Jesus!

EDGAR. Hey, what *is* this? Another game?

CAROL. Oh, Jesus! Oh, sweet Jesus!

SAM. Oh, hey! Wow!

FRED. What the fuck's going on!?

SAM. (*Hugging Carol.*) Oh, boy! Hey, we ought to work up an act!

CAROL. Oh, God, that was fun! (*She sees that Fred is not amused.*) Fred! Hey, Fred! (*She goes to him, hugs him.*) Hey, Fred!

FRED. (*He flings her arm away.*) It's all *right!* Just . . . it's all right. Let go of me!

LUCINDA. (*Rather sour.*) That was a joke. Is that it? (*To the audience.*) Is that what everybody's laughing about? That it was a joke?

SAM. (*Very pleased with himself.*) Yes, Lu; that was a joke.

LUCINDA. (*Ugly little smile; to Sam.*) I just want to keep up. I don't want to fall behind all you bright types.

EDGAR. (*Hugs her.*) Luuuuuuuuuu!

FRED. (*Trying to recover his dignity.*) That was very funny; you got a big rise out of me, and it was very funny; (*Indicates the audience.*) everybody had a good laugh.

SAM. Awwwww, Fred!

JO. (*Challenging.*) Including you, Fred?

FRED. (*Bluff.*) Sure! Sure! (*The others are silent.*) No! To be truthful, *no.*

CAROL. (*Sincere.*) Aw, Fred.

FRED. No! I rose to the bait, I took it, and I was hauled in. I was humiliated!

EDGAR. No! You weren't!

CAROL. Awwww, Fred!

SAM. You just showed you cared, Fred.

FRED. (*Heavily sarcastic.*) Yeah? Is that it?

CAROL. Yeah! That's it!

FRED. (*Shrugs.*) O.K. that's it. You saw me with all my clothes off.

JO. (*A half-smile.*) How come you don't hit somebody, Fred? This isn't like you.

FRED. Yeah; I know.

LUCINDA. (*Bright.*) Oh, that's interesting!

EDGAR. (*Really fed up.*) Why don't you just shut up, Lu? (*She glares at him for quite a while; he ignores her.*)

FRED. (*Ingenuous.*) Maybe I'm getting soft; maybe I like you guys.

SAM. Maybe you're in love.

FRED. (*Shrugs.*) Maybe I'm in love. (*To the audience.*) Maybe I'm in love.

JO. (*Into her glass.*) I wouldn't count on it.

SAM. Aw, come on, Jo.

FRED. (*To Carol.*) You gonna marry me, Carol? (*To the audience.*) Carol's gonna marry me one day.

JO. You gonna marry Fred one day, Carol?

CAROL. (*Appraises Fred; to the Others.*) I don't know. How many of us end up marrying Fred?

FRED. (*To the Group.*) Three, so far; I'm a three-time winner. You wanna marry me, Carol? Christ, now I'm asking her in public! Three-time winner, Carol; you wanna make it four?

CAROL. (*Very true, if nose-wrinkling.*) I don't *know*. (*To the audience.*) Really. I don't know.

SAM. (*To Jo.*) Four of a kind isn't bad.

JO. (*Shrugs.*) Beats a full house.

EDGAR. You gonna marry Fred, Carol?

CAROL. (*Quite pestered.*) I don't know, I don't know, I don't know! I know it's late and I got the itch, but beyond that I'm not sure.

FRED. I should drink up?

CAROL. Suit yourself; I've done it solo.

FRED. (*Sighing, rising.*) Maybe we ought to go, host and hostess.

LUCINDA. (*Rises, nudges Edgar.*) Well, we certainly are. Come on, Edgar.

FRED. (*Sits again.*) Oh, well, then, we'll stay.

SAM. (*To Lucinda and Edgar; only mildly protesting.*) Oh? You . . . taking off?

EDGAR. (*Reluctantly rising.*) Apparently.

JO. (*Moody; to the audience.*) Hardly anyone stays up late anymore. Why do you think that is?

21

LUCINDA. (*To Jo; a schoolmarm.*) It's because we all get tired earlier than we used to.

JO. (*Still to the audience; sags her shoulders; great, mock defeat.*) Oh, God! Do you think it's that!?

EDGAR. Thank you, Sam—especially for the games, all of 'em. (*To Jo; a concerned tone; light, though.*) You take it easy, Jo.

JO. (*To Edgar; toasts him.*) Alley-oop!

EDGAR. (*An arm around Sam's shoulder now.*) Night, you two; you suffer fools so gladly; it's a gift.

JO. (*Salutes Edgar.*) Help yourself, if there's any left.

EDGAR. Remember the alimony, Fred; remember the itch, but remember the alimony. (*Fred waves.*)

LUCINDA. (*Generally.*) Good night, now; good night. (*No one reacts. To the audience; quite peeved.*) No one says good night to me, you may have noticed.

JO. Nobody says good night to you? Not even Edgar?

LUCINDA. (*To Jo.*) Well, of course *Edgar* says good night to me!

JO. (*Deep chest tone.*) Well, then!

LUCINDA. (*Sort of hysterical.*) Of course, Edgar more or less *has* to say good night to me!

JO. Still! Count your blessings!

LUCINDA. (*Beady-eyed and tough.*) My cup runneth over, hunh?

JO. Right! But watch the rug.

EDGAR. Come on, Lu, let's get you out of here in one piece. Be good to one another.

JO. Any particular order we should do that in?

EDGAR. Nah; touch one, touch all.

LUCINDA. (*Eyes narrowing; to Jo.*) Just what did you mean by "count your blessings"? Just what did you mean by that?

EDGAR. (*Eyes to heaven.*) Oh, Christ!

SAM. What are you two going to do now, have a fight, or something?

LUCINDA. (*Clearly spoiling.*) No, we're not going to have a fight; I merely want to know what Miss Smartypants here means by "count your blessings," that's all.

EDGAR. Oh, Christ!

JO. (*Rising to it.*) All I meant *was*—my *dear* Lucinda—that you are lucky . . . that *anyone* . . . says good night to you, by which I su*spect* I meant . . .

SAM. Oh, God.

JO. (*Louder.*) By which I su*spect* I meant you're lucky you've got

22

anybody living in the same *house* with you, much less merely *talking* to you.

LUCINDA. (*Stiff; cold.*) I see.

JO. Is that *clear*?

LUCINDA. (*Nose out of joint.*) I think *so;* thank you very *much.*

JO. (*Drawl.*) Ooooooh, you're · welcome; my goodness, you're welcome.

EDGAR. Come on, Lu.

SAM. (*Quietly cajoling.*) Be *nice,* Jo.

LUCINDA. (*Grand, if stern.*) I'm going to forgive you, Jo.

JO. (*Deep tone again.*) Thanks, Lu.

SAM. Jo . . .

LUCINDA. (*None too kind.*) I'm going to forgive you because I assume the pain is very bad. (*A general silence.*)

JO. (*Sighs, stares at the ceiling.*) Well, nothing compared to the one you give me, Lu. (*Snarls.*) Get out of here, will you!?

LUCINDA. (*A brave smile; to the audience.*) Jo used to have at me this way when we were at college—making fun of me all the time. (*To the Others, now.*) It's become a habit; we don't even know we're doing it anymore.

JO. (*Pretending consternation.*) Gee, I thought *I* knew.

EDGAR. (*Pulls at Lucinda.*) Come on; get out of here before you're plucked clean.

LUCINDA. (*To Fred and Carol.*) She really doesn't know she's doing it.

EDGAR. (*Impatient with her.*) O.K.; O.K.! (*To Sam and Jo; drawled.*) Thank you, you two; it was your nice, average, desperate evening; we had fun.

SAM. So did we; so did we!

FRED. So did we!

CAROL. Yeah!

JO. (*Still pretending to be puzzled.*) I thought I *knew* I was having at her; I could *swear* I *knew.*

LUCINDA. (*Close to tears.*) Come on, Edgar; Jo's "tired."

JO. (*Mocking.*) "Jo's tired." Fuck off.

EDGAR. (*Gentle.*) Take it easy, Jo. Night, Sam.

SAM. (*Goes to the hall with them.*) Let me come with you.

EDGAR. No, no; come on!

JO. "Let me come with you." "No, no; come on." (*Calls after, too bouyant.*) Night! Thanks for coming! (*To Fred and Carol.*) Wanna keep me alive? Wanna cause a remission?

FRED. (*Smiles nicely.*) What do I have to do—kill Lucinda?

JO. That'd sure help. (*To herself, mostly.*) Wouldn't do any good, but it'd sure help.

CAROL. (*Trying to help.*) I lost a sister.

JO. What'd you do, leave her in the parking lot, or something?

CAROL. (*Tiny pause.*) Skip it. (*A silence; Sam reenters.*)

JO. Night? Thanks for coming?

SAM. *Is* it? *Is* it very bad?

JO. (*Transparent.*) What? Is what?

SAM. The pain. Is it very bad?

JO. (*A harsh laugh.*) It could be worse . . . they keep telling me. (*Shrugs.*) Nah; I just don't like her.

SAM. (*Gentle correction.*) C'mon; I know you.

JO. (*Dismissive.*) Change the record.

SAM. Look, I'm not one to complain . . .

JO. Good! Pull up a drink and sit down; join us.

FRED. Clear a space somewhere; c'mon in; the Scotch and water's fine.

SAM. (*Views the room; sighs.*) I don't know how six people can make such a mess of a perfectly good . . .

JO. Leave it. Let it pile up. (*Sam laughs, shrugs.*) Tired, baby?

SAM. Lots of things. Why do we ask them over, Jo?

JO. (*A child giving the correct answer.*) Because they're our friends, tha's why.

SAM. God, you're awful to Lucinda.

FRED. (*Feigned surprise.*) Jo? Awful? To Lucinda?

JO. (*By way of apology.*) Everybody's awful to Lucinda, except Edgar, maybe, and who knows?

SAM. No; everybody makes *fun* of Lucinda, but you're *awful* to her.

JO. (*Languid.*) Well, maybe we ought to even it out more. You want to be awful to her next time? How about you, Fred?

FRED. (*Helpful.*) Sure, I'll do it.

SAM. (*To Jo.*) Be careful; you may need Lucinda one day.

JO. (*Laughs.*) Who? Me? (*Detached.*) Well, I dare say the day will come I'll need you all. Then, of course, the day will come I won't need a soul. And then, of course, the day won't come.

SAM. (*Little-boy sad.*) Oh, Jo.

JO. (*To the audience, as above.*) That's what they tell us, isn't it—that growing pile of books on how to die? That somewhere along the line you stop needing those you . . . need the most? You loose

24

your ties? God, what do you need then? (*To Sam; some energy.*) Hey! Rub my shoulders.

SAM. (*Moves to her; begins.*) Why *do* we have them over, Jo?

JO. Why do we have *anyone* over? Less on the neck when I'm trying to talk, or is that the idea? Why do we have them over? Did I say because we love them?

SAM. (*Rubbing her shoulders.*) Nope; you said because they were our friends.

JO. (*Offhand.*) Oh. Well, add because we love them, but secretly mean because we need a surface to bounce it all off of . . .

SAM. I'm moving back toward the neck.

JO. I'm almost done. Because! Because it's too much trouble to change it all, and because we probably do love them in spite of everything . . .

SAM. (*Examining her neck.*) There's meant to be a pressure point, a nerve right about here on the neck . . .

JO. O.K.! O.K.! If you're going to ask me broody-type questions, don't expect me to be . . .

SAM. Lucinda isn't all that bad.

JO. Yes, she *is*.

FRED. She *is*, Sam.

CAROL. Oh, yes; she really is.

SAM. (*To the Three of them.*) She's no worse than Edgar for putting up with it—with *her*.

JO. What she's no worse than is your friend Fred, the floozy-bopper; that one over there.

SAM. What's the matter with Fred?

CAROL. (*Eyes narrowing.*) The what?

FRED. What's the matter with me?

JO. You're a pain; that's what's the matter with you.

CAROL. (*Assimilating it, with interest.*) The floozy-bopper?

SAM. What's Fred ever done to you?

FRED. Yeah. What've I ever done to you? (*Wiggles his eyebrows.*) 'Cept in my mind, maybe?

CAROL. Floozy-bopper? (*Grudging admiration.*) That's pretty good.

JO. (*Swings around to Fred.*) What have you done to me? You have subjected me to three—count 'em, three!—of what I assume is to be an endless parade of wives, each of whom is further from the mark than the previous one.

SAM. (*The peacemaker.*) Well, now he's got Carol.

FRED. And Carol's different.

SAM. And, besides, it's his business.

JO. Shut up! I'm being irrational! It is *not* his business; we have to put up with it. Besides, he's a reactionary, Nixon-loving fag baiter; he's . . .

FRED. Nobody's a Nixon-lover; nobody ever *was* a Nixon-lover; nobody even voted for him; ever! Don't you keep up?

JO. (*Grudging.*) Well, that's true. Still! I don't like you, Fred, when you get right down to it.

FRED. (*No help at all.*) I like *you.*

JO. (*Head back; Bernhardt.*) Oh, God! Oh, God! The burdens! (*Wriggles free.*) What are you doing? Fiddling with me? God!

SAM. (*Mild.*) The lady don't want to be coddled no more?

JO. Coddle me not. (*Afterthought.*) On the lone prairie. (*She rises, stretches, begins to move about; suddenly she is bent double with pain; she falls back on her footstool, her hands clutching her belly. She howls; it is a sound of intense agony and protest at the same time. It is not very loud, but profound. Sam stands where he is, watches. A silence; then she howls again; same nonreaction from Sam, though Carol covers her ears and leans in toward Fred, who cuddles her. Edgar has come back in during this last. He is framed in the doorway.*)

EDGAR. (*Into the silence.*) Please? (*Pause.*) Hello?

SAM. (*Great weariness; sighs.*) Hello, Edgar.

FRED. What did you forget, Edgar? Your youth? Your dignity, your—

EDGAR. (*Cutting Fred off.*) Neither; both; take your pick. Jo? (*He walks over to Jo; she looks up at him with pleading and pain; no sound, though. Softly.*) Jo, I came back because Lucinda is . . . because Lucinda is sitting out on the lawn, crying her heart out.

FRED. (*Sotto voce.*) On the lawn? (*Now, and during the rest of Edgar's following speech, Jo will howl from time to time, not very loud, but intense, as a counterpoint to his remarks.*)

EDGAR. (*A dismissing gesture to Fred; then.*) We get outside, Jo, and we start across the lawn, and she plops right down and she starts crying, right there. She says she can't take it anymore, Jo, the way you go at her; the way you make such terrible fun of her in front of everybody! She says it was all right until you got sick but now you're sick you mean it in a different way, and it's breaking her heart. (*She howls.*) Don't do that, Jo; I'm trying to *tell* you. Lucinda's down there on the lawn, and she's pulling up tufts of grass and throwing 'em around, and she's got dirt all over her, and

I don't think it's any crap: she means it; she's not going to get up from that fucking lawn 'til you say you're sorry. So I think you better get down there and help her—apologize, or what—in spite of your pain, because she's in pain down there, too, and she didn't cause yours. (*A silence.*)

JO. (*To the audience.*) Well, I don't suppose there's any answer to that 'cept get up and go down there with her—"sit upon the ground and tell sad stories"? (*To the Others now.*) Tear up a few mutual tufts, hold on to each other, rock, console? I guess I'd better.

SAM. No, Jo!

JO. Edgar's right: Lucinda's in pain. (*Jo rises, clearly still in some pain herself.*) OWWW! And pain is less fun than a few other things. Can I have a hand? (*She puts her hands out; Sam helps her up.*)

CAROL. You want your shoes?

JO. Nah, it's bedtime; besides, the grass tickles; I like it. Edgar? I'll set it right at best I can; no promises; your wife ain't easy; she can turn a kindly phrase sour in the best of mouths, but I'll try.

EDGAR. (*Sincere.*) Thank you, Jo.

JO. (*To Sam.*) Give Edgar a drink; give him some comfort; tell him some lies.

SAM. (*As they move toward the hallway.*) Easy. You're so light.

JO. I weigh nothing; I'm air. Off to the lawn.

FRED. We better go, too. C'mon, toots.

SAM. Be careful, Jo; it may be damp.

CAROL. (*Not too enthusiastic.*) O.K.

JO. You mean I may get a cold to go with the rest?

FRED. (*Moving to Jo, taking her from Sam.*) One strong arm.

JO. What's the matter with the other one?

FRED. Take it easy, lady.

JO. (*A laugh.*) What is all this—in case I fall? In case I become dust on the threshold?

FRED. Take her other arm, Carol.

CAROL. She can make it; she's a good girl.

JO. (*To Sam.*) I'm a good girl.

SAM. Come back, Jo.

JO. I'm a good girl. Who are you? (*Jo exits, with Fred and Carol.*)

SAM. (*To the empty hallway.*) You're a good girl; come back. (*Edgar stays standing; Sam doesn't look at him, but picks up a few glasses.*)

EDGAR. (*Finally.*) Do you want to talk?

SAM. Nope.

27

EDGAR. You want to make me a drink?

SAM. Nope.

EDGAR. Uh . . . you want to give me some comfort? You want to tell me some lies?

SAM. (*Almost laughing.*) Oh . . . go make your own drink.

EDGAR. (*An imitation: what? a girl?*) Gee, I thought you'd never ask.

SAM. (*Sitting.*) You *want* some comfort? You *want* some lies?

EDGAR. (*Looking.*) I want some bourbon.

SAM. Right in front of you. O.K., let's see: *you're* looking well; *Lucinda's* looking well; *Fred's* looking well; *Carol's* looking well . . .

EDGAR. (*Concentrating on his drink.*) Very funny.

SAM. *Jo's* looking well; *I'm* looking well . . .

EDGAR. (*Abrupt, but not loud.*) Can't you control her? Even a little? You let Jo just run wild these days, these nights?

SAM. (*Looks away; sighs.*) Yeah, I pretty much let her do what she wants to do.

EDGAR. (*Cool.*) You figure that's best?

SAM. (*Unintimidated.*) I figure that's best.

EDGAR. (*Pause; rather arch.*) Well, I suppose that's the way it ought to be. I mean, I suppose you should know.

SAM. (*Closing the subject.*) I suppose I should know.

EDGAR. (*Muted.*) I suppose you should. (*Pause; he slams his drink down.*) JESUS CHRIST, WHAT KIND OF A HOUSE DO YOU RUN AROUND HERE?

SAM. (*Too calm, if anything.*) Hm? Pardon me?

EDGAR. YOUR FUCKING GUESTS END UP CRYING!?

SAM. (*Still calm.*) They love us: they cry. Look to your own house, buddy.

EDGAR. (*Intense, but less loud than before.*) People don't cry at *our* house! People don't come over and visit *us* and go away sobbing!

SAM. (*Harsh.*) No! They go away laughing! Behind your back, of course, but laughing!

EDGAR. (*Clearly an old subject.*) Oh, Christ, not that again, hunh!? I am not you; Lucinda is not Jo; black is not white, and when the fuck are you going to get it all straight?

SAM. (*Shakes his head; mock consternation.*) I keep *trying;* I keep *trying.*

EDGAR. I *know* you don't like the way I run my marriage . . .

SAM. I didn't know you ran it.

EDGAR. What? I know you don't even *like* Lucinda, for that matter; *any* of you!

28

SAM. (*Mock shock.*) Oh! How did you ever figure that out!? We've kept it so . . . so . . .

EDGAR. (*Serene; even superior.*) But I don't *care*.

SAM. Oh, that's clear.

EDGAR. I decided a long time ago that the fact I love Lucinda gives her all the virtue she needs—if there's any lack to begin with. It's a common enough thing; we all do it; I just admit it.

SAM. (*Almost a sneer.*) Well, I dare say you'd have to.

EDGAR. (*Furious.*) You're no different!

SAM. (*Cool.*) Edgar, you're my only friend whose every virtue embarrasses me. You're the only man I know does something good and I want to hit him.

EDGAR. (*So reasonable.*) Well, I guess you *need* me, Sam.

SAM. I'm not into M and S.

EDGAR. S and M.

SAM. What?

EDGAR. (*Turning a little nasty.*) Yeah, I guess you need me. I mean, shit!, what's a martyr for 'less there's someone 'round the corner to do him in? Fred'd never turn on me: he's too straight-forward; Carol hasn't been around long enough to learn the game.

SAM. *Any* game.

EDGAR. What? Jo has her own problems, and so that just leaves you, ol' buddy. I don't need to take my shirt off, do I? You got a whip goes right through cloth, don't you? You say you're not into it?

SAM. (*Smiles; to the audience.*) It's the self-indulgence of these martyrs gets me most.

EDGAR. (*Smiles; to Sam.*) Is it? Does it? Glad you got it pinpointed. (*Pause; gentle.*) Can I help?

SAM. (*To Edgar; pause; shakes his head.*) Nobody can help.

EDGAR. Can *any* of us help?

SAM. Nobody can help.

EDGAR. (*Acknowledgment.*) Not even the village martyr.

SAM. Move *over*.

EDGAR. (*As above.*) Yeah; sure thing.

SAM. (*Looks up; tears, but no outburst.*) It's a death house I'm keeping here, old friend . . . to answer your question.

EDGAR. (*A silence.*) I know; and nobody can help.

SAM. No; nobody.

EDGAR. (*Helpless shrug.*) Right! (*Pause.*) I'll go see how they're doing.

29

SAM. You do that.

EDGAR. (*By the hallway.*) I'll even put the divots back. How's that for friendship? Hunh?

SAM. Pretty good. Not bad. (*Edgar moves to exit, but stops, listens as Sam begins. To the audience/to himself/to anyone.*) Each day, each night, each moment, she becomes less and less. My arms go around . . . bone? She . . . diminishes. She moves away from me in ways I . . . The thing we must do about loss is, hold on to the object we're losing. There's time later for . . . ourselves. Hold on! . . . but, to what? To bone? To air? To dust? (*Jo enters as Sam begins to weep. He lets his weeping develop, slowly, softly, toward a full expression of misery. His shoulders shake; he sobs; he lets it spend naturally. As he weeps, Jo replaces Edgar in the archway, Edgar exiting. Jo leans against the hall, observing Sam. He becomes aware of her presence; she becomes aware of this. He finishes his weeping notwithstanding.*)

JO. (*When he is about done; seemingly offhand.*) Don't cry; don't cry.

SAM. *You* cry.

JO. (*Begins to move about the room.*) Ah. Well. (*Afterthought.*) Women cry.

SAM. *Men* cry.

JO. (*A smile; apologetic.*) Yes, but if *you* cry, I will, *too,* and haven't I enough? I mean, if I started crying for myself, what would hold me together? (*She goes to him; strokes his head.*) Help me not to cry? Please? (*He buries his head in her crotch, his hands on her buttocks; he shakes his head slowly.*) Now; now; now.

SAM. (*Releases her; turns away.*) None of this is easy, you know.

JO. (*Small, sardonic smile.*) Your pain's as bad as mine, eh?

SAM. (*Angry at being misunderstood.*) I didn't *say* that!

JO. (*She too, angry.*) I didn't *say* you said that!

SAM. Of *course* it's not as bad as yours; it's not even like yours! What do you take me for?

JO. Husband?

SAM. But I *share* it.

JO. (*Strokes his cheek.*) No, you don't, and I'm glad. Yours is almost all in your head—in your mind, I mean—and mine isn't thank you, ma'am! (*To the audience.*) God! I wish it *was*—all in my head, in my mind.

SAM. (*To Jo, for her attention.*) You can't measure pain! I'm in pain! I love you!

JO. (*To Sam; comforting.*) I *know* you are; and I love *you.* (*To the audience again, with a harsh, abrupt laugh.*) Jesus, that would be funny!—if you could measure pain?

SAM. (*Crying again.*) Dear God, stop it! Please?

JO. (*Very gentle; almost lyrical; to Sam.*) All right. See? Stopped. (*To the audience; shrugs.*) Stopped. (*A silence. Jo takes a small pill vial from a pocket.*)

SAM. (*Sees it.*) How many today? How often are you . . . ?

JO. (*Ironic again.*) Popping the old pills? Oh, ten, twelve a day. Guess I better get myself down to ol' Doc Wheeler for a new prescription—or a stronger one.

SAM. (*Hollow.*) Ten or twelve?

JO. (*Laughter in the dark.*) Sure; why not!

SAM. A day?

JO. (*Deflated.*) Oh, come on.

SAM. God, Jo.

JO. (*A heavy sigh.*) Look, Sambo, you better get used to it. It's not going to get any less and it's not going to get any better. I'm up; I'm moving about; I'm engaged in what they refer to as social intercourse; I don't scream more than seven or eight times a day, on a good day . . . (*Sam covers his ears, hunches over.*) Don't cover up like that! It's *me* we're talking about! (*She pulls his hands from his ears.*) I say it's *me* we're talking about! Christ, if you can't take it now, what will you be like when I *need* you? *Really* need you!? (*Afterthought.*) Or something?

SAM. (*A truthful answer.*) I don't know.

JO. (*Far away.*) No. And I don't know what I'll need.

SAM. No. (*They both seem huddled and sort of lost.*)

JO. Well, give it some thought: the day *is* going to come. What did ol' Doc Wheeler say? Don't plan great distances ahead? Like, don't try getting your master's, or anything.

SAM. (*Softly.*) You have your master's?

JO. Hm?

SAM. You *have* your master's?

JO. I don't think he knows that; . . . what I think he *meant* was: wind it up; you're winding down, so . . . wind it up.

SAM. (*Glum; dogmatic.*) Everything is reversible.

JO. (*A vulnerable smile.*) Spontaneous combustion, or whatever they call it?

SAM. Mmm-hmmmm.

JO. But that's the localized ones, or the ones in the blood some-times . . .

SAM. (*Exploding.*) DON'T GIVE ME YOUR FACTS! YOU'RE SO PROUD OF YOUR FUCKING FACTS!!

31

JO. (*Calm and steady, to counter his outburst.*) I have a right to know what's going on, 'specially if it's going on in *me*.

SAM. Let it *go!*

JO. (*Leans in toward him; so dispassionate.*) Some day, when *you're* dying, when *that* day comes, when the day comes you're *told*, or the day comes you realize you've known but haven't admitted it, I would dearly love to be around.

SAM. (*Hurt.*) Jo . . .

JO. (*Winces a little: to the audience.*) That isn't *kind, is* it.

SAM. No.

JO. (*To Sam.*) No. There are two *theories* on that, you know—on being the first to go, or not.

SAM. Oh?

JO. Well, there are two theories on *everything*. One theory is that dying first is kinder—showing the way, and all, I suppose; none of this "after you" stuff. The other theory is that "staying on alone," is the gentlemanly thing to do—or the gentlewomanly, as the case may be.

SAM. Or . . . not doing it at all.

JO. Or . . . not doing it at all. (*Pause.*) Well, yes; *that* has something to be said for it.

SAM. (*Absurd and sincere.*) Please? Don't do it at all?

JO. (*A tiny pause; to the audience; for the sake of not letting a silence happen.*) In the *olden* days, in *some* societies, they would do it together—a hubby and wife, when one or the other was "going"— and in *Egypt*, now, they used to take the servants, and bury *them* along with . . .

SAM. (*Shocked wonder.*) Can't you stop?

JO. (*Looks at Sam, rather surprised to see him; speaks to him.*) I say, they used to bury the servants with their masters. 'Course, with the way help is today . . . I'm sorry, Sam; I'm really sorry.

SAM. (*Disgust?*) What kind of pills are you *taking*, for Christ's sake?

JO. Pain and sleep; pain and sleep. Got any *other* suggestions? No? (*Harsh laugh.*) They'll have me on heroin eventually. (*Sam moves behind her.*) Bet you never knew you were marrying an incipient dopie, did you; bet you never knew one day you'd have to— (*He claps his hand over her mouth, pulls her head to his body. She resists momentarily, then turns, puts her arms around his legs/hips. It is a reversal of the previous embrace. A silence.*)

SAM. (*So gentle.*) We just can't talk about it, it's that simple.

JO. (*Finally; subdued.*) There are two theories on that, too. Bet you

32

don't want to hear them. (*Sam shakes his head. Jo rises, moves off a little; Sam stays where he is.*) What was it? You do, or you don't?

SAM. No. No, I don't want to hear them.

JO. (*Shrugs.*) *Some*one's got to listen; *some*one's got to humor me.

SAM. I listen; I humor you.

JO. Not enough!

SAM. (*Sad and weary.*) Jo, you warn me not to humor you, and then you tell me I'm not . . .

JO. (*Doesn't want to hear it.*) I know!

SAM. You tell me to ignore you when you get like this, and then you yell at me for . . .

JO. I know! I know!! Don't . . . don't . . . just don't . . . (*Calms down.*) I've got to have it both ways. Don't pay any attention. Pay attention? Please?

SAM. (*Defeated.*) Whatever you want. (*A silence.*)

JO. (*Clearly whistling in the dark.*) Do you think you'll marry again, Sam? Who'll you marry?

SAM. Jo, I . . .

JO. Come on! Play!

SAM. Jo . . .

JO. Come one! Humor me! Who you gonna marry?

SAM. (*Hard.*) Carol; naturally.

JO. (*Chuckles a little.*) That'd upset old Fred.

SAM. Why? Does old Fred want to marry me?

JO. I can't speak for Fred, but if *I* were Fred, *I'd* marry you. (*Instinctively, they run to each other and embrace.*) Oh, my Sam, my Sam! I'd marry you in a minute!

SAM. (*Picks her up in his arms.*) Shhhh, shhhh, shhhh, shhhh.

JO. In a minute. (*Cuddled; protected; content.*) Am I heavy? No, of course I'm not heavy. What am I thinking of?

SAM. Shhhh, shhhh, shhhh.

JO. I think my sleepy pills are working. Shall I go to sleep right here? Can you stand there all night?

SAM. You're not *that* light. I'll take you up. (*He doesn't move, beyond kissing her neck.*) I'll take you to bed.

JO. (*Giggles contentedly, interrupted by a sudden spasm of pain, a sharp intake of breath.*) Giddyap!

SAM. Hm?

JO. Giddy*ap!* I think you'd better get me upstairs right now. I need a couple of more pills.

SAM. (*Standing still, cuddling her.*) Not sleepy enough?

JO. Oh, I'm plenty sleepy, but if I start in screaming . . .

SAM. (*Galvanized.*) O.K.! O.K.! Right! (*He starts with her toward the stairs.*)

JO. (*Clearly in pain.*) Don't jiggle me! I think I'm all coming apart! AaaaaaaaaaahhhhhhHHHHHHH!! (*This is a cry of beginning and rapidly growing sudden pain.*)

SAM. (*He starts up the stairs with her.*) O.K.! O.K.! (*Jo grabs at the banister, leaves Sam's arms. He hovers above her.*)

JO. AaaaaahhhHHHH!! Sweet Jesus!! AaaaaaaHHHHHHHH!!

SAM. (*Helpless.*) Let me help you.

JO. AaaaaaannnnnnNNHHH! (*She waves him off.*) In a minute. (*Very heavy breathing.*) AAAAARRRrrrrrrrrrrrrgggggggHHHHH! God! God! God! Try to lift me! (*Sam tries.*) Haaannnnh! (*He has her on her feet again. This next through heavy breathing and gulping.*) It's . . . been . . . easier to . . . get me . . . to bed . . . before.

SAM. (*Gently taking her to the top of the stairs; soothing, crooning.*) I'll take care of you now; I'll make you better; you'll see; I'll put you right to bed, and take a cold cloth to your . . .

JO. (*A harsh laugh that is also a jolt of pain.*) Just . . . get me up there and lay me down. Haaaannhhh!

SAM. Sh, sh, sh. Easy, now; easy. (*They vanish from the landing. Silence for a moment. Jo howls Offstage; then again, louder; then again, pathetic. Silence again. Elizabeth and Oscar enter the set from one side, from without the set, in that order. Oscar is dressed in a suit and tie; Elizabeth is dressed elegantly. Elizabeth sees the audience, puts her finger to her lips, lest they start commenting, or applauding, or whatever.*)

OSCAR. (*Looking about, with some distaste.*) You say this is the place?

ELIZABETH. (*To the audience, not urgent, not languid, but no nonsense.*) Is she alive? Are we here in time? (*The sound of Jo's scream from upstairs; a brief silence, then another scream. Elizabeth, still in the audience, her eyes acknowledging the sound with a brief, upward movement of her head.*) Ah yes! Well, then; we *are* in time. (*Turns her head slightly toward Oscar.*) Yes; this is the place.

CURTAIN

ACT TWO

Morning. Elizabeth alone Onstage, looking out the bay window, maybe. Sam comes down the stairs, just awake, still in his sleeping gown; he does not see Elizabeth; he sees the remains of the party's mess; he takes a few more glasses, etc. As he does this, Elizabeth hears him, turns, sees him. He sees her.

ELIZABETH. (*A smile; steady.*) Good morning.

SAM. (*A long silence. Finally, not loud.*) Who are *you?*

ELIZABETH. It was *late* last night; you'd already gone upstairs; there seemed no point in . . .

SAM. (*Still not loud, but more persistent.*) Who *are* you?

ELIZABETH. There seemed no point in calling you back down don't interrupt me, *please;* there seemed no point, from the . . . sound of it, so to speak. So, I did not, or, *we* did not, to be more accurate.

SAM. W-we!? (*Looks about swiftly, sees no one.*) Who *are* you!?

ELIZABETH. Do you always leave your lights on? Glasses about? I straightened up for you a bit. If you have a fire going, do you . . . abandon it, and hope for the best? Civilizations have gone down that way, you know.

SAM. (*Teeth clenched now.*) Who *are* you!?

ELIZABETH. Look at Russia! Carelessness; putting off; no other reason for the Bolsheviks. If the Czar and his boys had been a little quicker, a little more precise, Lenin wouldn't have had a chance. He'd have stayed in Zurich and taken a job teaching at some university.

SAM. (*Overly polite.*) Who *are* you?

ELIZABETH. Probably would have gotten tenure—if they had tenure in those days. Don't you think it's ironic Karl Marx was a Jew?—the Soviets being so anti-Semitic, and all?

SAM. I don't believe he had Russia in mind. WHO ARE YOU!?

ELIZABETH. You don't believe he had . . . ! Is that so! (*To the audience.*) Of course! It was probably Germany he had in mind all along, and if it had worked out the way Marx and Engels had it planned we would have been spared both Hitler and Stalin. Good

35

old Marx! Good old Engels! (*Back to Sam.*) Or, do you think we would have had Hitler and Stalin anyway, in some other guise—the "we-get-what-we-deserve-no-matter-what" theory? I'm of two minds.

SAM. (*Losing patience, but still understated.*) Who are you?

ELIZABETH. Which is an odd phrase, is it not: "I'm of two minds." (*A shift of tone to more serious, concerned.*) It sounded pretty awful up there last night. The pain, I mean. It sounded . . . well, relentless.

SAM. (*Rage coming.*) Who *are* you!? (*To the audience.*) Who *is* this woman?

ELIZABETH. You'll be on injections soon—*she* will be, rather. I hope you're prepared for all that—man into nurse; overseer; the diminishment. I hope you're prepared for all that.

SAM. (*To Elizabeth; threat deep in the throat.*) Who AAARRRRE you!?

ELIZABETH. (*This speech to both Sam and the audience.*) I remember someone, a lady who had been good to me, a lady much older than I, older than I am now and I was young; I remember there was no one else to do it all; it was on *me;* I didn't like any of it: injecting, swabbing, bathing, changing, holding close, holding her close to crush the pain out of her; picking her up—my God, no weight at all, a sack of dust-picking her up to take her to the window, so the roses and trees could get a look at her, I guess; and taking her back. "Where are you taking me," she said. "Where did you take me to, and where are you putting me?" Her eyes were open; she'd gone blind with it and I hadn't known. She hadn't said—or noticed. (*To Sam alone now.*) I wonder who she was? Was she my mother? I hope you're prepared for it.

SAM. (*Finally.*) WHO ARE *YOU!!!???*

ELIZABETH. (*So calm.*) You're shouting. Who *am* I? (*To the audience.*) The gentleman wans to know who I am. (*To Sam.*) Well . . . who are *you?*

SAM. I'm Jo's husband; this is my house . . .

ELIZABETH. You'll wake her with your shouting. Is she still asleep? You'll wake her.

SAM. (*A quick glance above; intense, whispered.*) Dear, great God, woman, who are you!?

ELIZABETH. (*Quietly amused by Sam's phrasing.*) Dear, great God, woman, who am I? (*Oscar enters from the library.*) Oscar? Who am I? (*To Sam.*) This is Oscar; Oscar and I are . . . together. (*Sam swings around to face Oscar, who bows his head slightly, smiles. Sam stiffens, takes a few steps back, to have both of them in view.*)

OSCAR. (*To Sam.*) Good morning, young man. (*To Elizabeth.*) Who *are* you? Well, ooze my widda wubby cupcake, is what-'ums *ooze* is.

ELIZABETH. (*Laughs.*) Widda *wubby* cupcake? What's a wubby?

OSCAR. (*Great dignity.*) A wubby? A wubby is an adjective. (*To Sam.*) I said: Good morning, young man.

ELIZABETH. (*Some disbelief.*) An adjective?

OSCAR. (*To Sam.*) It was late last night; you'd already gone upstairs; there seemed no point in calling you back down. (*To Elizabeth.*) Yes; an adjective, as is widda; widda and wubby are both adjectives.

ELIZABETH. It *seems* . . . excessive.

SAM. (*Quiet threat.*) I want you both out of here—whoever you are.

OSCAR. (*To Sam; unintimidated.*) Do you always leave your lights on? Glasses about? If you have a fire going, do you . . . abandon it, and hope for the best?

ELIZABETH. We've *done* that. He pointed out, by the way, that Marx and Engels didn't have Russia in mind at all.

OSCAR. (*Broad, to the audience.*) Well, everyone knows that.

ELIZABETH. (*Quarrelsome.*) Not *every*one. I'm sure there are perfectly good people, walking upright and all, who have never heard of Marx and Engels—Engels certainly.

OSCAR. (*To Elizabeth.*) Impossible! A ridiculous idea!

SAM. (*Flat.*) Carol.

OSCAR. Hm? Pardon?

SAM. Carol; she didn't know who Marx and Engels were.

ELIZABETH. There! You see!? A perfectly good person.

OSCAR. Who says! (*To the audience.*) Who is this *Carol,* and who do we know of her? Is she to be trusted? Would she *pretend* not to know who Marx and Engels were? (*Sam is moving toward the telephone slowly, keeping his eyes on them both. To Elizabeth.*) Is she the sort of person who would get *pleasure* from appearing stupid?

ELIZABETH. Not Carol. Not if I know Carol.

OSCAR. *Do* you know Carol?

ELIZABETH. (*Shrugs, giggles.*) *I* don't know. Show me Carol, and I'll tell you. (*Sam moves to the phone, begins dialing.*)

OSCAR. (*To Sam.*) Who are you calling? The police? What will you tell them? What will you tell them we are? Thieves? Murderers? Relatives come to call? House inspectors? What? (*Sam hesitates, hangs up.*)

ELIZABETH. *House* inspectors?

37

SAM. (*Curiously close to tears.*) Will you *please* leave?

OSCAR. You don't even know who we *are* and you want us to leave. (*To Elizabeth.*) *House* inspectors: that's the people who inspect houses. (*To Sam again.*) Don't you want to know who we are?

SAM. (*Explodes.*) No! No, I don't want to know who you are! I want you out of here! I want you out of here now! (*Looks toward the ceiling, points.*) Damn it! My wife is very ill . . .

OSCAR. (*To Sam.*) Well, why else are we here? (*To the audience.*) Oh, I suppose there could be other reasons: a ride in the car; a breath of fresh air; a look at how the neighborhood's changed; the thrill of expectation—all that.

SAM. (*Suspicious.*) You know Jo?

OSCAR. (*To Sam.*) Why would we come here if we didn't *know* someone? What do you think we are?

SAM. (*Not to be put off.*) You know her? Tell me how you know her.

OSCAR. (*To Sam.*) Look here; do you think we're house inspectors? Do we *look* like house inspectors? (*No reply.*) Well, maybe you don't know what house inspectors look like. They wear hats; they carry cigars; they tend toward overweight; you can turn their heads with a twenty, or a kiss. Why are you wearing that strange garment? (*Sam becomes aware of how he is dressed.*)

ELIZABETH. I rather like it.

SAM. (*Iron.*) It's how I dress; it's how I dress for bed.

OSCAR. Ah, then you're going to bed.

SAM. I've *been* to bed.

OSCAR. Ahhhh. Then you've just gotten *up*?

SAM. (*Irritated.*) Yes!

OSCAR. (*To the audience.*) *I've* been up for hours; I rarely sleep.

ELIZABETH. (*To the audience.*) I dozed; I watched the night die. (*Pause.*)

SAM. (*Fairly assertive.*) Leave!

OSCAR. (*To Sam.*) What did *you* do?

ELIZABETH. (*To Sam.*) Did *you* sit up? We heard the cries, and then the silence. Did you sit up, and hold her hand until the drugs had done their work? Did you lie down beside her then, put off the light, and stare up into the dark? Where did you fall asleep? Where did you wake up? Hm?

SAM. (*Softly.*) Please? Leave?

ELIZABETH. (*As softly; comforting.*) No.

OSCAR. (*Bright; after a pause.*) Since we are not house inspectors, nor have ever been, and, for that matter—though I speak for

38

myself—cannot imagine being, then we are thieves, murderers, or . . . relatives come to call.

SAM. *Please!*

ELIZABETH. Be gentle, Oscar.

OSCAR. Are you very wealthy? If we are thieves, after all . . . (*Looks about. To the audience; wrinkles his nose.*) "Comfortable," I should think, as the definitions go. Not much ostentation, but *still* . . . a little too obvious for "old money," wouldn't you say? No battered greatness. (*Back to Sam now.*) Where are your animals? Very rich people always have livestock. No, you're comfortable, nothing more.

SAM. (*Heavily sarcastic.*) Sorry!

OSCAR. (*Spies a print on the wall.*) What is that!? (*Goes to it. To the audience.*) My goodness; a Jaspar Johns! (*To Sam again.*) None of that Warhol shit for you, eh? Good taste! A nice print.

SAM. Take it!

OSCAR. What! A print!? Don't be silly.

SAM. Take whatever you want. Take the stereo; take the television; there are *three* of them, take 'em all!

ELIZABETH. Why?

SAM. Pardon?

ELIZABETH. Why are there three TVs? There aren't enough programs for one. What happened, did they just . . . accumulate?

SAM. (*Shrill.*) I'm not going to apologize for having three TV sets! Get out of my house!

OSCAR. (*To Sam.*) She wasn't suggesting you should; be calm. We don't *want* your gadgets; next you'll offer us a microwave oven, or a Cuisinart. Your stereo and all that stuff are for junkies and for punks. *Look* at us; we don't even want your nice little Jaspar Johns. We're not *thieves.* Are you relieved?

SAM. (*Very unpleasant; an edge of threat.*) No!

ELIZABETH. Nobody would offer a Cuisinart to a pair of thieves—punks *or* junkies; you're being outré.

OSCAR. (*To Elizabeth.*) Well, if I were a *thief,* that would be something I would *know.* (*To Sam.*) Which proves what I said—that we are not . . . thieves.

SAM. WHAT *ARE YOU!?*

OSCAR. Well, from the original list that leaves murderers and relatives come to call.

ELIZABETH. Not necessarily a happy choice—though I don't know your circle.

SAM. WHAT THE FUCK DO I HAVE TO DO TO GET YOU OUT OF HERE!!?? (*A silence.*)

OSCAR. (*Quietly.*) Guess who we are, for beginners. And you're so close.

SAM. (*Sits; rather defeated.*) All right; who *are* you? Who *are* you?

OSCAR. (*Going to him; gentle.*) We are not murderers, nor are we thieves . . .

ELIZABETH. Nor are we house inspectors . . .

OSCAR. (*The end of a fairy tale.*) Then we are relatives, come to call.

SAM. (*Weary.*) You're relatives; good. You're . . . (*Looks at Oscar.*) . . . no, you're not! You're not a relative at all!

OSCAR. Oh?

SAM. (*Gestures.*) Well . . . *look* at you. (*Elizabeth chuckles throughout.*)

OSCAR. *Look* at me? Am I dressed oddly? Do my clothes offend?

SAM. (*Knows what's being done, but can't fight it.*) No.

OSCAR. Am I too tall?

SAM. No.

OSCAR. Too *short.*

SAM. No; no.

OSCAR. Am I too old?

SAM. No.

OSCAR. (*Feigning confusion.*) Too young?

SAM. No, of course not.

OSCAR. Too thin, then.

SAM. No!

OSCAR. Too fat?

SAM. NO!

OSCAR. Is it my way of speaking? Am I too . . . refined?

SAM. NO!

OSCAR. Am I . . . too rich?

SAM. How would I know?

OSCAR. Too poor?

SAM. How would I *know!*?

OSCAR. Well, it *is* a puzzle. What could it *be?* Could it . . . oh, my goodness, I think I have it! Is it . . . (*He leans over and whispers in Sam's ear.*)

SAM. (*Listens, nods.*) Yup; that's it; you got it.

OSCAR. (*To Elizabeth; mock distress.*) It's that I'm . . . (*Stage whisper.*) Too black.

ELIZABETH. (*Absurd!*) Too what! Too black!?

OSCAR. It would appear so.

SAM. No offense.

OSCAR. Given or taken? (*To Elizabeth.*) It would appear so. Too black. What did Mister Blake say? . . . "But I am black, as if bereav'd of light." (*Hamming.*) "And, I am black, but, oh, my soul is white!" Some shit like that.

SAM. I said: no offense.

OSCAR. And none taken, white boy; none taken. Well, now, if I am too black to be a relative—though there's a nigger in many a woodpile, and don't you forget it!—then *I* must be a *friend.* Perhaps Elizabeth here is a relative.

SAM. (*Almost a mumble.*) Well, I'm sure Jo will be very happy to see you.

ELIZABETH. (*To Sam; arch.*) Was that sarcasm? (*To Oscar.*) Oscar, did that sound like sarcasm to you, to your black ears?

SAM. (*Weary.*) It was not sarcasm.

OSCAR. It sounded like it to me. (*Smiles unpleasantly. To the audience.*) But then, so much does.

SAM. (*Frustration, fatigue.*) It was *not* sarcasm; I'm very *tired;* I sat *up;* I'm sure Jo will be very happy to *see* you. God! Let it *go!*

OSCAR. (*Rather cheerful; to Sam.*) Be nice to this lady; she has come a distance.

SAM. (*Trying to be conversational.*) What, uh . . . what kind of relative . . . uh, *are* you?

ELIZABETH. (*Surprised, but gracious.*) Why . . . I'm Jo's mother. (*Considerable pause.*)

SAM. (*As if he hadn't heard properly.*) Pardon?

ELIZABETH. (*Patient.*) I'm Jo's mother.

OSCAR. (*To Sam, when he fails to respond.*) Her *mother!* Jo's *mother!* (*Sam begins to laugh, quietly, shaking his head; the laughter is close to crying. To Sam.*) Is that the laughter to keep from crying? (*To Elizabeth; chipper.*) Do you think that's the laughter to keep from crying?

SAM. (*A heavy sigh.*) O.K. gang; out! Whoever you are . . . get out.

ELIZABETH. (*Rather harsh.*) I'm Jo's mother, come from Dubuque!

41

OSCAR. The Lady from Dubuque; this is the lady from Dubuque; Jo's mother!

ELIZABETH. (*A hand up.*) Never mind, Oscar.

OSCAR. (*To Sam.*) Jo's mother; from Dubuque. What's the *matter* with you!? *Kiss* her!

SAM. (*Anger through the fatigue.*) You are *not* Jo's mother. (*To the audience.*) She is *not* Jo's mother. (*To Elizabeth and Oscar.*) JESUS CHRIST, HAVE SOME COMPASSION, WILL YOU!?

OSCAR. (*Very offhand; to the audience.*) I wonder why he's resisting?

ELIZABETH. (*Sighs; rises.*) I wonder why we're *talking?* Clearly it's no use. It's time I went upstairs.

SAM. (*Frightened, but standing his ground.*) You're both crazy; both of you, you're crazy.

ELIZABETH. (*Dismissing him with a little gesture.*) Oh . . . fiddlesticks! Oscar, will you stay down here with this young man?

SAM. YOU STAY AWAY FROM JO!!

ELIZABETH. (*Amused.*) Stay away from her? Not let her hug me? Where do you think she learned it all? Do you think she put her arms around nobody before *you?* What gall! We all have antecedents, and we all can be replaced. Keep that in mind.

SAM. You stay away from her!

ELIZABETH. Why don't you be a good boy and go in the kitchen now and make us all a hearty breakfast?

OSCAR. (*Wringing his hands; smacking his lips.*) Corn pone, grits . . .

ELIZABETH. A Sunday breakfast! Steaming pots of coffee, rolls, and eggs, and slabs of ham. Jo used to love that, back on the farm.

SAM. (*Contemptuous.*) You were never on a farm in your life.

OSCAR. (*Almost to himself.*) Iowa *is* farm country.

SAM. (*To the audience; desperate.*) Jo's mother lives in New Jersey!

ELIZABETH. (*After she and Oscar both hoot.*) New Jersey!? Do you mean this person you're trying to pass off as Jo's mother comes from . . . New Jersey?

SAM. What are *you* . . . some kind of *comic?*

ELIZABETH. (*Suddenly very sober.*) No; very serious, and very concerned. Will I find the bedroom to the right? (*She starts toward the stairs; Sam moves to a blocking position.*)

SAM. You stay where you are.

ELIZABETH. (*Stone.*) I have come home for my daughter's dying. Get out of my way.

SAM. (*An almost-whispered litany.*) You are not Jo's mother, you have never been on a farm, Jo was not raised on a farm, you are not from Dubuque; you are not a relative and this black man is not a friend.

ELIZABETH. This black man here, who is probably very rapidly becoming what you say—*not* a friend—is wise and quick and shockingly strong.

OSCAR. (*Smiles.*) Imperial Japanese Army; World War Two.

ELIZABETH. I think he will help me if I need him.

OSCAR. (*Mock ecstatic.*) Oh, Elizabeth! Anything!

SAM. (*Kind of punchy.*) You were *not* in the Japanese Army in World War Two.

OSCAR. (*To the audience.*) I wonder where I learned my love for uncooked fish?

ELIZABETH. Not to mention your command of the martial arts. (*To Sam, with a charming smile.*) He'll have you unconscious just like that.

OSCAR. (*Bows in the Japanese manner; to Sam.*) Ohayoo gozaimasu. Ogenki desuka? (*Sam doesn't respond.*) Do shimashita ka? (*To Elizabeth.*) What's the matter with *him*?

ELIZABETH. (*Shrugs.*) He doesn't know Japanese; he's lost face. (*To Sam.*) Don't fret; it's not a required language yet. Just like that! Unconscious, flat on your back. *So-o*, if you will let me pass . . . (*Sam blocks the stairway; Oscar moves slightly; Sam includes him in his defense posture—arms angled in front, hands as barriers, eyes flickering from one to the other.*)

SAM. (*Steel.*) Stay away from me, you crazy people!

OSCAR. (*Karate pose; to Sam.*) HIIIIIIIIIYYYYYEEEAAAAA-HHH!!!

SAM. Oh, my *God!*

ELIZABETH. (*Purring.*) Would you care to negotiate, young man?

SAM. (*Not taking his eyes off Oscar.*) Would I care to . . . would I *what?*

ELIZABETH. You have a woman upstairs. You *say* she is your wife; *I* say she is my daughter. Surely we can negotiate this.

OSCAR. (*A sinister echo.*) Surely you can negotiate this.

SAM. (*Quietly; to Elizabeth.*) Who *are* you? *Really?*

ELIZABETH. (*Gentle.*) Who are *you? Really?* (*A long silence; Sam looks at them both.*)

43

SAM. (*Finally; very calm.*) I'll go upstairs, and I'll talk to Jo. I'll wake her if she's asleep, and I'll tell her what's been happening; she won't believe me, but I'll tell her.

ELIZABETH. Bring her down.

SAM. (*Adamant.*) I'll *tell* her.

ELIZABETH. (*Harder.*) You'll bring her down; that's our negotiation. Negotiation's over; I'll call off the dogs. (*She turns her back on Sam.*)

OSCAR. (*Quite amused.*) You'll call off the *what?*

ELIZABETH. (*Laughs.*) Oh, hush!

SAM. If she says she'll come—if she believes what I tell her and she says she'll come—maybe you'll be gone. You aren't really here, are you? I'll come back down and you'll be gone?

OSCAR. Gone?

ELIZABETH. (*A harsh laugh.*) Oh, *we* exist. Worry about your*self*.

SAM. (*Starts backing up the stairs.*) *I* exist; *you* don't.

ELIZABETH. (*Lazy.*) Well, we'll see. (*Amused.*) Oh! While you're up there . . . *do* change out of that silly getup.

SAM. (*Near tears.*) It's how I dress; it's how I dress for bed! (*He hesitates, then rushes up the stairs and Offstage.*)

ELIZABETH. (*Convulsed.*) It's how I dress! (*To the audience.*) It's how I dress for bed! (*They both laugh greatly; Elizabeth holds her hands out, palms upward; Oscar slaps them in an exaggerated imitation of street blacks. Their backs are to the entry hallway.*)

OSCAR. (*To Elizabeth; sober.*) He doubts you. (*To the audience.*) He doubts her.

ELIZABETH. (*To Oscar; to herself.*) I know. (*To the audience.*) How can he doubt me? How can he doubt me? (*Lucinda and Edgar enter from the hallway, Lucinda leading the way.*)

LUCINDA. (*With enthusiasm.*) Surprise! Surprise! Sur . . . (*She sees Elizabeth and Oscar, finishes it, deflated and cautious.*) . . . prise; surprise.

EDGAR. Well . . .

LUCINDA. (*To Elizabeth.*) Good . . . good morning.

ELIZABETH. (*A grand hostess.*) Good morning; I'm Jo's mother . . . and you must be . . . ?

LUCINDA. (*Nonplussed; self-conscious.*) Jo's . . . what? Jo's mother? (*Fairly faint.*) I'm Lucinda and this is Edgar.

EDGAR. (*Uncomfortable.*) Hi.

ELIZABETH. (*Grand.*) How do you do? This is Oscar. (*Oscar bows.*) Oscar is black.

LUCINDA. I noticed.

EDGAR. Yes; so did I. (*More formal.*) Where's Sam? Where's Jo?

ELIZABETH. (*Rather offhand, if final.*) They are . . . upstairs.

EDGAR. (*Puzzled.*) Thank you.

LUCINDA. (*Nervously, to fill the gap.*) So. You're Jo's mother.

ELIZABETH. Yes; I am.

LUCINDA. I never would have guessed! I mean . . . you're not at all what I imagined.

ELIZABETH. Oh?

LUCINDA. We've never had the pleasure, of course—you're something of a recluse; a famous name in these parts, but nothing more.

ELIZABETH. Oh?

LUCINDA. (*Not helped by Elizabeth.*) You . . . you live with your *sister* now.

ELIZABETH. I . . . move about all the time.

LUCINDA. (*Confused.*) Oh?

ELIZABETH. (*A short laugh.*) Well! One may *be* from Dubuque . . .

OSCAR. Iowa; Dubuque, Iowa.

LUCINDA. Du . . . buque?

ELIZABETH. But certainly one *roams:* Dubuque is not everything.

LUCINDA. (*Puzzled.*) Sam says you live with your sister, couple of hours from here. (*With an uncomfortable look at Oscar.*) With your older sister; you two sort of . . . look out for one another.

ELIZABETH. (*Laughs.*) Sam says that? (*To Oscar.*) What can Sam mean?

LUCINDA. (*To Edgar; uncertainly.*) I'm sure that's what we've been told?

OSCAR. Sam's a joker all right.

LUCINDA. (*Quite puzzled.*) You never go out; you stay in. (*Nudges Edgar.*) Edgar! Help me! (*A nervous laugh.*) And you're very tiny, and terribly thin.

ELIZABETH. (*Crystal laughter.*) You must have me confused with someone else—a great aunt, perhaps. I have my Christmas in Switzerland, though, to be completely candid with you, I spent *one* December in Peru.

LUCINDA. Pe . . . ru?

OSCAR. (*Helpful.*) The country.

LUCINDA. And . . . and you have pink hair.

45

ELIZABETH. (*Greatly amused.*) Pink hair!? On purpose?! (*To the audience.*) Pink hair!?

OSCAR. Clearly you have Elizabeth confused in your mind with someone else—some defective or eccentric somewhere, some embarrassment your friends are taking care to see is . . .

LUCINDA. (*Close to hysteria.*) Well, I must be mistaken! Edgar? Jo's mother is clearly not a recluse; I mean . . . *look* at her: she does not have pink hair, nor is she tiny.

EDGAR. No.

OSCAR. (*Mollifying.*) She's not . . . gigantic, of course.

LUCINDA. No! We can *see* that!

OSCAR. She is what you might refer to as a normal-size mother.

LUCINDA. Yes! Yes! Still . . .

EDGAR. Oh, come on, Lucinda! For Christ's sake!

LUCINDA. (*Making ineffectual little slaps at Edgar.*) Don't *be* that way to me! Give me one good reason why Sam, or *Jo—Jo,* for heaven's sake—give me one good reason why Jo would pretend her mother is a tiny, pink-haired recluse, living—

ELIZABETH. *BECAUSE!!* (*Silence; attention is paid. Quietly; to end the matter.*) Because . . . there are things you would not be expected to understand. (*A long silence.*)

EDGAR. (*Finally.*) Right.

LUCINDA. Oh. (*Pause.*) All right; if you say so. (*To save it.*) Besides, I knew it wasn't true from the beginning—New Jersey, pink hair, and all!

EDGAR. (*To Lucinda; humoring her.*) You get everything so mixed up! Can't put one over on you, eh Lu? (*Lucinda starts to reply, but Fred and Carol appear in the hallway.*)

FRED. (*Just as he comes into view, Carol following.*) Hey? Anybody up?

OSCAR. (*To the audience.*) My gracious! It *is* a party!

FRED. Anybody . . .

EDGAR. Fred! For Christ's sake!

FRED. (*Takes it all in.*) . . . hey, what's all this!

ELIZABETH. (*Still the grand hostess.*) Good morning! I'm Jo's mother, and you must be . . . ?

FRED. (*Some urgency; to Edgar.*) Where's Sam? Where's Jo?

EDGAR. It's O.K. They're upstairs.

FRED. (*To Lucinda and Edgar.*) What the hell are you two doing here?

CAROL. (*Peering at Elizabeth and Oscar.*) We in the right house, Fred?

FRED. (*Not really unpleasant; preoccupied.*) Shut up, Carol.

ELIZABETH. How do you do!—whoever you may be.

CAROL. I don't think we're in the right house, Fred.

FRED. (*To Edgar.*) What the hell are you two *doing* here?

EDGAR. Lucinda wanted to make it up with Jo . . . for last night . . . out on the lawn.

FRED. Oh.

ELIZABETH. And you? (*To the audience.*) Don't these people answer questions?

FRED. Hunh?

ELIZABETH. (*Too precise; to Fred.*) And . . . you! To what do we owe the pleasure? Are you friends of my daughter as well?

CAROL. (*To Fred; sotto voce.*) Is that Jo's *mother?*

FRED. Shut up, Carol. (*To Elizabeth.*) Well, Carol here and I, we decided to get married—you know, what the hell!—and so we wanted to tell Sam and Jo, and . . .

ELIZABETH. Well, well; congratulations.

EDGAR. How *about* that! Hey!

CAROL. (*Shrugging twice.*) You know: what the hell!

LUCINDA. (*Badly disguised distaste.*) Oh; you two are getting married; how wonderful.

FRED. Ah, fuck off, Lucinda.

LUCINDA. (*Defend me!*) Edgar?

EDGAR. Do what Fred says, hunh? (*To Fred and Carol.*) That's swell, kids; that is just swell.

OSCAR. (*To the audience.*) I haven't heard "swell" in a very long time. Can you remember when you last heard "swell"?

ELIZABETH. (*To Fred and Carol.*) This is Oscar. Oscar is black.

FRED. (*None too pleasant.*) I noticed. How come your friend is black?

ELIZABETH. How come he's what?

FRED. Black.

ELIZABETH. Black!? (*To Oscar.*) How come you're black?

OSCAR. Because my mammy and my pappy was black.

CAROL. (*A smile.*) Fred's a redneck.

ELIZABETH. (*To Carol.*) Isn't that nice? (*To Fred.*) Have you been one long?

FRED. (*A cold smile.*) It comes and goes.

OSCAR. (*To the audience; quite chummy.*) I met a foreign lady once —Belgian, I think—nice lady, very solicitous, kept asking me questions about something she insisted was called the Ku-Ku-Klan. Nice lady. (*To Fred; very pleasant.*) Are you a member of the Ku-Ku-Klan?

FRED. (*Tight smile.*) What do you want to bet?

CAROL. Aw, come on! Fred's a pussycat. (*Oscar laughs, unpleasantly. A silence.*)

LUCINDA. Jo's mother here has come all the way from Dubuque to pay Jo a visit, Jo being sick and all . . .

FRED. Dubuque?

ELIZABETH. I am from Dubuque; I am the lady from Dubuque. (*Specifically to Edgar.*) Though I have not just come from there. I was in . . . uh . . . (*Clearly she's improvising.*) St. Paul de Vence, on my way from Paris down to . . .

OSCAR. (*Right in.*) Rome; Rome, Italy.

ELIZABETH. Thank you. (*To the others.*) I do not . . . summer in Dubuque.

CAROL. (*An aside, to Fred.*) Who is this *person?*

LUCINDA. (*Effusive.*) Jo's mother is not at all what we had been led to believe.

ELIZABETH. (*To Fred and Carol.*) Tiny, pink-haired, reclusive, living on the dole somewhere with a sister.

LUCINDA. No; well; you *see!* Not at all what we'd imagined. The idea of Sam leading us on like that . . .

CAROL. (*Merely curious.*) Are those pearls real?

ELIZABETH. Real what?

CAROL. (*Hostile.*) Real pearl!

FRED. Shut up, Carol.

CAROL. (*Quite angry, but not loud.*) Don't tell me to shut up all the time. You want me to marry you? Just come off it about shut up all the time. We aren't married *yet*, so *watch* it!

ELIZABETH. (*Gracious.*) I don't know; they were given me; but I've no reason to assume they're other than that which they pretend to be. (*Sam has appeared at the top of the stairs; he has changed into a shirt and trousers.*)

SAM. Unlike some people I could mention.

FRED. Hey! Sam! (*Sam slowly descends the stairs.*)

LUCINDA. (*Nervous; sing-song.*) You're having a *party!* You may not have *known* it, but you're having a *party!* Fred and Carol are getting—

FRED. Hey, Sam, you hear about Carol and me? We're getting married.

EDGAR. Morning, Sam.

ELIZABETH. I've been entertaining your friends; they're charming, absolutely charming. Oscar and I have been enthralled.

CAROL. (*Sheepish.*) Hi, Sam.

LUCINDA. We've gotten to know Jo's mother here. We were so surprised; we came in, more or less on tiptoe, and . . .

FRED. Carol and I are getting married, Sam. (*Sam is at the bottom of the stairs now. He has not taken his eyes off Elizabeth the entire journey down. He stops in front of her.*)

OSCAR. (*To Elizabeth; cooing.*) See how he loves you already; he can't take his eye off of you.

FRED. Sam? You O.K.?

EDGAR. Sam?

OSCAR. (*To the audience.*) See how he stares at her! See the intensity of his gaze! *This* is passion!

FRED. (*Concerned.*) Sam?

SAM. (*Waves them off; to Elizabeth, precise, quiet, formal, controlled.*) I spoke to Jo; I told her . . . you two had arrived; I told her who you said you were.

ELIZABETH. And?

SAM. She's getting up; she's coming down; and that will be the end of it.

LUCINDA. (*To Edgar and Carol.*) I don't understand what's going on!

EDGAR. Sam? You O.K.?

SAM. It's . . . (*Bravura; slightly hysterical.*) . . . it's all right, folks, it's . . . all . . . just wonderful. This . . . this lady here and her—and this one—the two of them were waiting for me when I came downstairs this morning. *This* one—this lady here—says she's Jo's *mother.* I don't know who *this* one thinks *he* is. *I* say she's *not* Jo's mother.

FRED. (*Laughs.*) Oh, come on, now!

SAM. No, now! Don't laugh!

FRED. (*Harsh laugh.*) *Nobody* pretends to be somebody's *mother!*

SAM. (*Contained, but the hysteria is underneath.*) I know! Nobody pretends to be somebody's mother!

(*Still the hysteria underneath; to Fred, Carol, Edgar, Lucinda, and the audience.*) THIS IS NOT JO'S MOTHER!

FRED. (*To Sam; sighs.*) O.K., Sam, what are you doing—playing some kind of game? Didn't you have enough last night? What kind of game are you *playing?*

SAM. (*To Fred; sputtering; exploding.*) Am *I* playing! What kind of game am *I* playing!?

FRED. You got a sick wife upstairs, her mother comes home—with a friend, or something—and all you can do is make jokes?

SAM. (*Beside himself.*) All I can do is . . . ? THIS IS NOT JO'S *MOTHER!!*

FRED. Of course it's Jo's mother! Who the hell else is it!?

SAM. (*About to burst.*) I don't know! I don't *know* who it is!

FRED. (*Weary of it, dismissing Sam.*) Oh, for God's sake!

SAM. I DON'T KNOW WHO IT *IS!* (*A silence.*)

LUCINDA. (*Brisk; slaps her knees.*) Well! Who's for a good pot of coffee?

FRED. Fuck that! Let's open the bar. (*He moves toward the bar.*)

SAM. (*Fury.*) NOBODY!! (*Pause.*) NOBODY!!

OSCAR. (*Into a silence; to the audience.*) Well, I suppose that's natural—a man who would deny his wife's own mother could not be expected to provide his friends with a cup of coffee or a drink.

SAM. (*Turns to Oscar, fist cocked.*) Look, you fucker!

OSCAR. (*To Sam; loud, authoritative.*) I warn you! (*Sam hesitates; Oscar assumes a karate pose.*) I warn you; I have my black belt. (*An aside, to Elizabeth.*) Which should come as no surprise. (*Oscar holds out his palm; Elizabeth slaps it, in an exaggerated imitation of street blacks.*)

SAM. (*Turns away in disgust and defeat.*) Ah, for Christ's sake!

CAROL. (*To Sam.*) Your mother-in-law's quite a card; so's her friend there. (*To Elizabeth and Oscar.*) You're quite a pair.

ELIZABETH. (*Queen Elizabeth.*) *Thank* you, *thank* you.

SAM. (*Weary; ironic.*) You're quite a pair, too, Carol, but she isn't my mother-in-law.

LUCINDA. (*Dismissing him.*) Oh, really, Sam.

SAM. (*Hopeless.*) She's *not.*

FRED. Bullshit!

SAM. (*To Carol.*) You really gonna marry that sonofabitch?

CAROL. (*Argumentative, if not enthusiastic.*) He'll *do!*

SAM. Which says as much about you as it does about him! Congratulations to you both!

FRED. (*Quietly; to Sam.*) Fuck yourself; and no kidding. Just go fuck yourself.

ELIZABETH. (*Amused; above it all.*) Bicker, bicker! This is not the *time* for it.

SAM. (*To Elizabeth; enraged.*) You! You shut up!

FRED. (*Disgust.*) Look, this is a nice lady you're talking to.

SAM. (*Loud; looking down at the floor.*) SHUT UP! SHUT UP! SHUT UP! (*Jo appears at the top of the stairs. Suddenly shaken and in tears, pathetic.*) Please! Please! All of you! Shut . . . up! Just . . . shut . . . up. Please! (*A silence.*)

OSCAR. (*To the audience.*) The view from above, to the pit below.

ELIZABETH. (*Gentle, deferential.*) The man has asked for silence; give it to him.

OSCAR. (*Hands out, fingers wide; still to the audience.*) Let there be silence; shhhhhhhhhhh.

JO. (*Tentative.*) Sam?

SAM. (*A whisper.*) Jo? (*All eyes go to Jo. Elizabeth moves slightly so that she is near the foot of the stairs.*)

JO. (*As Sam makes to move toward her.*) No; I'll make it down; don't anyone move. (*She begins her descent, her eyes on Elizabeth. Halfway down she gasps in pain, nearly crumbles.*)

SAM. JO!

JO. (*Straightening again; smiling.*) No one *help* me. (*Jo completes her descent, save two steps; her eyes are still on Elizabeth; she stops where she is.*)

ELIZABETH. (*Gentle; a smile.*) Good morning.

JO. (*After a pause; quiet, noncommittal.*) Good morning.

OSCAR. (*To Elizabeth, his eyes on Jo.*) You never told me how lovely she was—so pure, so fragile: scented air.

SAM. These are the two who have come, Jo. This is the woman claims to be your mother. Tell her, Jo; tell her you don't know her.

ELIZABETH. (*Gentle.*) Good morning.

SAM. Tell her she has no right to come into our house and pretend to be what she is not. (*Jo has a spasm of pain; she moans.*)

LUCINDA. (*True grief.*) Oh, Jo!

OSCAR. Take her in your arms, Elizabeth; ease her; hold her close.

SAM. (*To Oscar.*) YOU STAY OUT OF THIS!! (*Jo grimaces; a cry escapes her.*)

ELIZABETH. Come to me.

SAM. (*Through his teeth.*) You stay away from her!

JO. (*Looks at Sam; quietly.*) Sam?

SAM. (*Begging.*) Tell her, Jo. Tell her we don't know her. (*Jo's eyes return to Elizabeth.*)

ELIZABETH. Come to me, now. It's time to hold you close, to rock you in my arms.

JO. (*Timid.*) Rock me?

ELIZABETH. (*Soothing.*) Hold you, rock you, take you to my breast.

SAM. NO!

ELIZABETH. (*A litany.*) Come, let me stroke your forehead, comb your hair, wash you, lay you down and tell you stories . . .

SAM. JO! NO!

ELIZABETH. Protect you from the dark and from the thunder?

JO. (*A little girl.*) Protect me?

SAM. NO!

ELIZABETH. (*Smiles.*) From the dark and from the thunder.

JO. Make it better?

SAM. (*Agony.*) Oh, Jo!

ELIZABETH. (*So tender, gentle.*) Make it better? What have I come for? Come to me.

SAM. (*A howl of pain.*) NOOOOOooooooOOOOOO! (*Finally, with tears and a great helpless smile, Jo rushes into Elizabeth's arms; their embrace is almost a tableau, so involved is it with pressing together.*)

ELIZABETH. (*To the audience.*) And they wonder who I am.

SAM. (*To his friends.*) No! NO! That is not Jo's mother! Believe me! BELIEVE ME!! (*But they have either turned away, are looking away in embarrassment, or are regarding Sam with sadness.*) NO! NO! (*He looks about and sees it is hopeless, but he persists, in rage and tears.*) NO! (*Pause.*) NO! (*Pause.*) NO!

OSCAR. (*Quietly; gently.*) Oh, yes. Yesyesyesyes. Oh, yes.

SAM. (*Fully in tears; quietly, desperate; to the audience.*) Believe me; this is not Jo's mother.

OSCAR. (*Quiet victory statement, to Sam.*) Oh yes she is.

SAM. (*In a final attempt to reverse the situation; to Elizabeth.*) NO!! (*Sam lunges at Elizabeth, to wrest Jo from her. As quick as lightning, Oscar intercedes.*)

OSCAR. (*Grappling with Sam.*) I said . . . YES! (*To Fred and Edgar.*) Help me with him! (*Jo cries out in pain. Fred and Edgar come to help. Sam and Oscar: overlapping.*)

SAM. No! No!

OSCAR. Yes, I said!

SAM. No! Jo!

OSCAR. Hold him for me. Hold him. (*Fred and Edgar each grab one of Sam's arms. Oscar touches Sam on the neck and he is instantly unconscious.*)

OSCAR. Ease him down. (*Sam, unconscious, slips to the floor.*)

EDGAR. How did you do that? (*Fred ties Sam's hands behind him with his belt.*)

OSCAR. There is a nerve there, in the neck; a little pressure in the proper spot . . . and all the woes are gone, the troubles slip away . . . and peace descends. Off you go, to the dreap and deemless.

EDGAR. Will he be all right?

OSCAR. He'll be all right. I can wake him . . . (*Finger snap.*) . . . just like that.

FRED. (*Having tied Sam up.*) I tied him up.

OSCAR. You did!? So you did. Those are splendid knots. Really first rate. He must be *very* grateful to you.

FRED. Bastard hates me.

OSCAR. (*Mollifying.*) Weeeellll, you've tied him up very nicely, nonetheless. A regular package.

FRED. (*None too pleasant.*) That's not a bad idea: *mail* him somewhere.

OSCAR. (*Bright idea!*) We could send him to New Jersey! He could visit those mysterious ladies.

LUCINDA. (*Amused.*) It would serve him right—hitting away like that!

EDGAR. (*To Elizabeth; truly puzzled.*) God, the way he just . . . went at you.

LUCINDA. I've never such a thing! Really! (*To Elizabeth.*) Weren't you scared?

ELIZABETH. (*Rather startled.*) Scared!? Why, no.

FRED. He was afraid to go after . . . (*Gestures.*) . . . this one here.

EDGAR. Well, with good reason! (*To Oscar.*) Where did you learn all that . . . (*Imitates Oscar's judo.*) . . . all that . . . ?

OSCAR. Foreign Legion.

EDGAR. You were in the Foreign . . . ? No.

OSCAR. (*Shrugs.*) All right. (*To the audience.*) Then I *wasn't* in the Foreign Legion. *I* don't care.

JO. (*A spasm alerts her.*) What's happening? What's . . .

ELIZABETH. (*Soothes.*) Shhhhhh; shhhhhhhh; nothing. (*Jo becomes comatose again.*)

FRED. (*Regards Sam.*) I think he looks good this way. Perfect packaging.

CAROL. (*Snorts; shakes her head.*) Hunh!

FRED. What's the matter with *you*?

CAROL. Sooner or later you're going to have to untie him, you know.

FRED. Yeah? So?

CAROL. (*Shrugs.*) Sooner or later you're going to have to untie him; or Jo's going to get with it, and you're going to have to let him *go*.

FRED. SO!?

CAROL. So . . . *then* you're going to have to explain why you tied him up!

FRED. (*Exasperated.*) I tied him up . . . you saw why I tied him up!

LUCINDA. (*After a crystal laugh.*) Really, Carol!

EDGAR. (*Puzzled.*) Who should we have tied up, Jo's mother here?

CAROL. (*A small smile.*) Who?

JO. (*An echo.*) Who?

ELIZABETH. (*A bit loud.*) Tied *me* up!? Why me? (*To the audience.*) Why would anyone tie *me* up?

OSCAR. (*Generally.*) Perhaps she meant *me*. (*To the audience.*) People are always tying coons up for one reason or another, though less *these* days than . . . (*Smiles.*) . . . times of yore?

CAROL. (*Speculative; not giving an inch.*) Well, it *could* be because I'm crazy . . .

FRED. Yeah! It could be because you're crazy!

CAROL. (*Dubious.*) Yeah; could be; or it could be because I'm an outsider . . .

FRED. So why don't you shut up?!

CAROL. (*Pursuing her logic.*) Or maybe it isn't either one; maybe it's just a feeling. Why are you all in such a rush? Why doesn't anybody believe *Sam*?

LUCINDA. (*Laughs.*) Oh, really, Carol!

FRED. (*Furious.*) For Christ's sake, why don't you just . . . go into the kitchen and make some coffee, or something!? Why don't you do something useful around here?

54

CAROL. What am *I!*? Some sort of a colored maid, or something? (*To Oscar.*) No offense.

OSCAR. (*To Carol; smooth.*) Oh, none taken!

FRED. (*As Carol doesn't move.*) Will you get your ass in there!?

CAROL. O.K.! O.K.! For Christ's sake! (*She sweeps out, muttering.*)

FRED. Good girl, Carol; just gotta goose her a little bit.

OSCAR. (*To the audience.*) And I haven't heard *that* word, *either,* in a coon's age.

FRED. (*Eyes narrowing a little.*) What word? Girl?

LUCINDA. (*Slaps her knees, rises.*) I'll make toast; I'll make buttered toast.

ELIZABETH. (*To Lucinda.*) That will be heaven. (*Lucinda smiles, exits.*) Won't that be heaven, Oscar?

OSCAR. (*Considers it; to Elizabeth.*) Well, it will be *toast.*

FRED. (*At the bar again.*) You drinking, Edgar?

EDGAR. No thanks, Fred; not this early.

FRED. (*Pretending to be offended.*) Oh, I see; well; pardon *me.*

EDGAR. (*For fear of having offended.*) Of course. I'm not getting married.

FRED. Oh? Why not?

EDGAR. Because I'm already . . . I just don't want a drink, Fred.

FRED. (*To Elizabeth and Oscar.*) I don't suppose either of you drinks in the morning, either.

OSCAR. No, no.

ELIZABETH. Certainly not.

FRED. (*Moves over to Sam, contemplates him.*) You want a drink, Sambo? A little Scotch with a straw? Sniff it, maybe? (*To Edgar.*) Sambo doesn't seem to answer.

EDGAR. (*Glum.*) Well, maybe *he's* not getting married, *either.*

FRED. (*Cheerful.*) Well, *I* am. Fuck ya all! (*Toasts.*)

JO. (*Dreamy.*) Who's getting married?

ELIZABETH. Fred is; Fred's getting married.

FRED. (*Loud.*) I'm marrying Carol, Jo.

JO. (*Thinks, shakes her head.*) Terrible idea. (*Subsides. Lucinda appears in the hallway, spoons in hand.*)

LUCINDA. Edgar! Come help with the tray! Don't be a bump! (*She revanishes.*)

EDGAR. (*Fairly weary; rises.*) O.K. O.K.

ELIZABETH. A what? A bump?

55

EDGAR. (*Exiting.*) As in on a log; a bump on a log; I shouldn't be a bump on a log.

OSCAR. (*In the small silence as Edgar exits; to the audience.*) Quaint.

JO. (*To Elizabeth; in confidence.*) I've told Fred a dozen times, I've been subtle, but I've told him—"Don't marry Carol."

ELIZABETH. Shhhh, shhh, shhh.

JO. And I've told Carol—"Don't marry Fred." Maybe nobody ever heard me; maybe nobody listens. I hurt.

ELIZABETH. Let me hold you.

JO. Fred is a terrible person.

ELIZABETH. (*Smiles, to Fred, shrugs.*) Shhh; let me hold you.

JO. He is . . . (*She smiles at her phrasing.*) . . . unworthy of human solicitude. (*Gasps.*) I really *hurt.*

FRED. (*Slams his drink down.*) I gotta go take a dump! (*He starts out.*)

ELIZABETH. (*Calm.*) Do you say that to offend us?

FRED. (*Daring her.*) What!?

ELIZABETH. (*Will not be drawn in; smiles.*) Or is it anger? Has Jo made you angry, and are you going to punish us all? Are you a showoff, or a boor, or is Jo right on the mark, and are you . . . "unworthy of human solicitude"?

FRED. I'm just plain dirt common; ask Jo. (*He exits.*)

OSCAR. Well, he is nothing if not honest, eh? (*Oscar wanders.*) Are you happy with the decor?

ELIZABETH. (*Casual.*) I would do something else about the carpet, I think, or put rugs down. How's the library?

OSCAR. Very masculine—heavy leather, dark woods. What would you expect? Oh! The TV set has doors, which close; they match the other wood.

ELIZABETH. (*Delighted; giggles.*) It doesn't! They don't! (*To Jo.*) Oh, Jo! You are a *good* girl!

JO. (*Vague.*) What have I *done?*

ELIZABETH. You're a good wife. You make a beautiful home. (*Carol enters.*)

OSCAR. Very good, "Mother," very good.

ELIZABETH. *Do* be a help.

OSCAR. What more can I *do?* I am civil to people I cannot abide, I function as an encyclopedia . . .

CAROL. You knock people out.

OSCAR. (*Recovering nicely.*) I knock people out.

ELIZABETH. (*Bright.*) My goodness, aren't you quick! Coffee all made?

CAROL. Too many cooks. Where's Fred?

ELIZABETH. (*Hesitates just a split second.*) I can't bring myself to tell you.

CAROL. (*Shrugs.*) He can't be far: I'm still here.

OSCAR. (*He smiles, too.*) You hold yourself in high regard.

CAROL. (*Matter-of-fact.*) No: accurate regard. I'm not your dumb brunette for nothing. (*Laughs.*) Do you know I'm a natural blonde? I dye it brunette 'cause I look cheap as a blonde? I look cheap natural?

ELIZABETH. (*Delighted.*) You don't! Are you really!? (*To the audience.*) Isn't that extraordinary!?

CAROL. (*To get Jo's attention.*) Jo!?

ELIZABETH. (*Protective; to Carol.*) Hsshhh! Don't bother her!

CAROL. JO!?

JO. (*Stirs, looks vaguely about to see who's calling her.*) Hm? What?

CAROL. (*Louder.*) JO!?

JO. (*Focusing on Carol.*) What . . . what's happened?

CAROL. (*Points at Sam.*) Take a look over there; take a look at Sam.

JO. (*Looks over at Sam for quite a long time; turns to Elizabeth; sort of dreamy.*) Why is . . . why is Sambo all . . . asleep?

ELIZABETH. (*Sweet.*) So he'll be nice; he wasn't being nice.

JO. (*Almost interested; sort of sad.*) What happened?

ELIZABETH. (*A look at Carol; to Jo, a secret.*) He wasn't happy with the way things are. He wanted everything back the way it never was.

JO. That's not nice.

ELIZABETH. No; it isn't.

CAROL. (*Eyes to heaven.*) Jesus!

JO. (*Sort of lost.*) I don't understand.

ELIZABETH. (*Pulls Jo to her, head to lap.*) You rest now.

CAROL. (*Matter-of-fact.*) Sooner or later you're going to have to wake him up.

ELIZABETH. (*Laughs.*) Well, of course!

OSCAR. Certainly you don't imagine we've thought of this as a . . . final solution.

CAROL. (*No nonsense.*) Who *are* you?

ELIZABETH. (*Grand.*) I beg your pardon?

57

CAROL. You can come off it for me; I don't count; I'm an outsider. Who are you, *really?*

ELIZABETH. (*Observing Carol carefully.*) Oscar, the natural blonde is suspicious.

OSCAR. I noticed.

CAROL. Sam says . . .

ELIZABETH. Sam says! Sam says!

OSCAR. What does Sam know? (*To the audience.*) What does Sam know? Sam only knows what *Sam* needs.

CAROL. *Sam* has rights, you know.

OSCAR. (*To Carol.*) And what about what Jo needs? What does what Sam needs have to do with that?

CAROL. (*Dogmatic, if uncertain.*) Things are either true or they're not.

OSCAR. Oh? Really? (*To the audience.*) Really? (*Fred enters.*)

FRED. (*To Carol.*) What'd they do: throw you outta the kitchen?

CAROL. (*Curiously angered.*) Where the fuck have you been?

FRED. (*Prissy and overarticulating.*) Powdering my nose.

CAROL. Whyn't ya untie Sam?

FRED. (*To Oscar.*) You gonna keep him like this all day? Whyn't you wake him up?

OSCAR. Really? (*To Elizabeth.*) Shall I?

ELIZABETH. Try. See what happens.

OSCAR. (*Shrugs.*) All right. (*He wakes Sam up.*) Voilà!

SAM. (*At once; as loud as possible.*) HELP!? HELP!? HELP!? HELP!? (*Etc., until Oscar's slaps—below—stop him.*)

FRED. Jesus!

OSCAR. (*To Fred.*) You see? I told you. (*To Sam, slapping.*) Now! . . . you! . . . stop! . . . that! (*Sam gasps, sobs a bit, subsides.*)

FRED. (*Shakes his head.*) Jesus!

SAM. Help me? Someone?

OSCAR. Behave yourself!

SAM. (*Softly; in his throat.*) Someone? Help me?

JO. (*An echo.*) Help me; help me.

SAM. Carol, can you . . . ?

FRED. (*Unpleasant.*) Carol isn't here to *help you.* Keep your hands off him, Carol.

JO. (*As above.*) Help me; help me.

SAM. Fred? Please?

CAROL. (*To Sam; kind.*) Fred isn't here to help you either. I don't think *anyone* is. (*Lucinda and Edgar reenter, Lucinda leading the way; they have trays—cups, plates, coffee, toast, marmalade, etc.*)

LUCINDA. My gracious, what yelling! What's going *on?!*

EDGAR. (*Slightly embarrassed.*) Coffee; coffee, everyone.

LUCINDA. What's going on!!?

SAM. (*Softly.*) Help me? Help me, please?

EDGAR. (*Puts his tray down.*) Hey, Sam; hey, boy!

SAM. God, Edgar, help me?

LUCINDA. (*To the audience.*) What's going *on!?*

EDGAR. (*To Oscar; to Fred; to them all.*) You gonna untie him now?

OSCAR. We woke him and how did he repay us: he shrieked to raise the very dead.

ELIZABETH. (*Softly.*) The very dead; who hear nothing; who remember nothing; who are nothing.

EDGAR. Was that Sam?

LUCINDA. (*Still to the audience; delighted.*) Was that Sam? Was all that yelling Sam?

CAROL. Getting off on it, Lu?

LUCINDA. (*To Carol.*) Pardon?

SAM. Edgar!? Help me!

LUCINDA. Leave Edgar alone; *you* don't love Edgar; you don't love anyone.

EDGAR. (*More sad than sarcastic.*) Oh, he loves me, Lu: I'm the only man he knows does something good and he wants to hit; I am his only friend whose every virtue embarrasses him.

SAM. Oh, God, Edgar!

LUCINDA. We don't forget, Sam; we forgive, but we don't forget.

OSCAR. (*To Sam; cheerful.*) I like your friends. (*To the audience.*) I like his friends.

CAROL. (*Matter-of-fact.*) *I'll* untie him; I don't know him; I'm not his friend; I'll untie him.

FRED. Keep your fucking hands off him.

CAROL. 'Cause I'm not his friend?

LUCINDA. It's getting cold. Who will have what? I know about you, Edgar.

EDGAR. (*Offhand.*) I don't want any.

LUCINDA. (*Pours for him.*) Don't be silly.

FRED. I'm a lush, Lu; don't give *me* any coffee.

LUCINDA. (*Furious.*) You *asked* for coffee! You yelled at Carol!

FRED. (*Waving Lucinda off; dismissing her.*) I wanted her out of the room; I wanted her to shut up; fuck your coffee. (*Afterthought.*) Fuck *you*, for that matter.

LUCINDA. (*Defend me!*) Edgar?

ELIZABETH. (*Half to break into the argument.*) I will have mine with white sugar and real cream; and if that stuff is instant take it all back into the kitchen and pour it down the drain.

SAM. (*Intense; a supplication.*) The coffee is not instant, the sugar is white and the cream is real, I have no friends, please let me go.

CAROL. If you're a lush, why should I marry you?

FRED. (*Another dismissing wave.*) You'll marry worse. I'm not so bad.

OSCAR. (*To Elizabeth and generally; taking Elizabeth her coffee and toast.*) "The coffee is not instant, the sugar is white and the cream is real." Here you are, my dear. "I have no friends, please let me go." Really!

ELIZABETH. Thank you. You spilled! You sloppy man!

OSCAR. (*Indicates Lucinda.*) *She* spilled; I wouldn't spill.

LUCINDA. (*Enraged.*) *I* didn't spill! I *never* spill! *You* spilled!

OSCAR. (*A calming tone.*) Very *well;* you didn't spill; no one spilled; there has been no . . . spillage. Spillage?

ELIZABETH. (*Shrugs.*) Why not?

SAM. Please? Untie me? Let me go?

LUCINDA. Carol? Cream and sugar?

CAROL. (*Her attention on Sam, etc.*) Nah; I don't want your coffee.

LUCINDA. (*A little laugh.*) It is not . . . *my coffee.*

EDGAR. (*An edge to his voice.*) No one *wants* it, Lu!

OSCAR. (*Dusts his palms.*) I'm going up. (*He moves toward the stairway.*)

SAM. (*Helpless suspicion.*) Where are you going!?

OSCAR. Up.

SAM. Don't *go* up there!

OSCAR. There's no one upstairs. What can you possibly mind?

SAM. (*Enraged by both the constraint and the action.*) DON'T GO UP THERE!!

EDGAR. (*Mild; rational.*) Why are you going up there?

OSCAR. (*Considers it as he takes a few more steps up; smiles.*) Because I've never *been.*

SAM. (*Trying to break loose.*) YOU HAVE NO RIGHT!!

JO. (*Vague.*) Who? Who has no what?

CAROL. (*Softly; to Oscar.*) You *don't* have any right, you know.

60

OSCAR. (*To Elizabeth; laughs.*) Tell them. Tell them all. Give them a reading about rights. (*Starts up again; to audience.*) Christ, these people! (*He disappears into the upstairs hallway.*)

CAROL. (*Shrugs.*) No right at all.

FRED. What are *you* going to be, a troublemaker?

CAROL. (*A gentle dismissal.*) Annnnh, go back to your boozing; don't worry about me; I'll fit in; it'll just take a while.

SAM. (*To himself; head down, shaking it.*) No right; no right at all.

ELIZABETH. (*Putting down her cup; to Sam; rational.*) These . . . these rights; these rights people do not have.

SAM. (*Slowly meeting her eyes.*) Yes?

LUCINDA. (*An aside, to Edgar.*) Did he really say that to you? That he wanted to hit you?

EDGAR. Shhhhhhh.

ELIZABETH. (*Pleased that Sam is meeting her eyes.*) Are these rights rights *no* one has . . . or, merely some?

LUCINDA. (*As above.*) What's she talking about?

EDGAR. SHHHHHHH! Jesus!

SAM. Merely some.

ELIZABETH. Aha! Then, there are rights which *you* possess . . .

SAM. In this *house!*

ELIZABETH. . . . which are yours alone!

SAM. In this house!

ELIZABETH. (*Smooth.*) Good; then we are not talking about the rights we pretend we give ourselves in this bewildered land of ours—life, liberty, and the pursuit of the unattainable—though we *may* be learning our limits—finally—here in the . . . last of the democracies. Or just about.

LUCINDA. (*Offended.*) The *last!*

ELIZABETH. Oh . . . probably; we're too moral to survive. A *real* Nixon will come along one day, if the Russians don't.

LUCINDA. (*Disgusted.*) You're a cynic!

ELIZABETH. (*Truly bewildered.*) *Am* I!? Dear God!

SAM. I have my *own* rights! My own personal rights! Jo! Pay attention to me!

ELIZABETH. *Have* you? What—this house? Jo? Surely you don't mean property—nothing as crass as that. Is it dignity you have in mind? (*To the audience.*) I had a dog named Dignity once—or, that was her name when I got her; I changed it; I called her Jane. She's dead. (*To Sam.*) Is it Jane you have in mind? Is it dignity?

SAM. Jo!? Please!

61

ELIZABETH. It is *not* Jane you have in mind; it is Jo.

JO. (*Vague.*) Me?

ELIZABETH. Back on the farm, when I was growing up, back on the farm in the outskirts of Dubuque . . .

SAM. (*So weary.*) You did not grow up on a farm; you did not grow up on the outskirts of—

ELIZABETH. Will you let me finish the story!?

FRED. (*Pointing at him with his glass; not nice.*) Sam, you shut up and let her talk.

SAM. Get out of my house.

EDGAR. Take it easy, Sam.

SAM. Get out of my house! *Both* of you! *All* of you! *All* of you get out!

JO. (*Far away.*) Did you want something, Sam?

ELIZABETH. (*Patient.*) Back on the farm, in the outskirts of Dubuque . . .

SAM. (*At the top of his lungs.*) OUT?! OUT?! OUT?! OUT?! (*Etc. During this, Fred puts his drink down, walks over to Sam, punches him hard in the stomach; Sam doubles over as best he can; gasps.*)

FRED. (*To Sam.*) You don't throw people out of *any*where, you superior bastard. We'll leave when we're finished. (*Pause; generally.*) I'm finished. (*He turns to go; to Carol.*) You coming?

CAROL. (*A sneer.*) Whyn't you wait around and see if you killed him?

EDGAR. Christ, Fred.

FRED. (*Of Sam; to Carol; oddly enraged.*) *Look* at him! *He's* alive! *Look* at him! (*Indeed, Sam is gasping.*)

EDGAR. Sam?

FRED. YOU COMING!? I SAID I'M GOING. YOU COMING!?

CAROL. (*Pause; calm.*) I think I'll have a cup of coffee before I go. Lucinda, I think I'll have a cup of coffee after all. (*Fred moves to the coffee service, sweeps it to the floor.*)

JO. (*Faint; at the sound.*) Oh; oh.

FRED. There's no more coffee. (*Between his teeth.*) You coming?

CAROL. I'll stay for a little; I'll help clean up the mess.

FRED. (*Pause; cold.*) I'll wait for you in the car.

CAROL. (*Nods.*) O.K. And if you're not there when I come out I'll go on over to the apartment; and if you're not there . . . (*Shrugs.*) . . . well, I'll just marry somebody else.

FRED. (*Pause; equivocal.*) I'll wait in the car. (*He turns; exits. A pause. Lucinda goes to the floor, begins to clean up.*)

EDGAR. (*To Carol; gentle with disbelief.*) You gonna marry that man?

CAROL. (*Looks at him; no emotion.*) You think of any reason why I shouldn't?

EDGAR. (*As Carol moves to help Lucinda; thinks.*) No, no, I guess not.

LUCINDA. (*Loss.*) All the pretty cups and saucers.

CAROL. (*To Edgar.*) I didn't think so. (*To Lucinda.*) Hey, here's one isn't broken . . . Yes, it is.

EDGAR. You O.K., Sam?

SAM. Sure, Edgar. My wife is dying; I am invaded; I am abandoned by my friends. But you really don't care how I am, Edgar; you didn't raise a finger.

LUCINDA. Don't you have at Edgar that way!

EDGAR. (*Quietly raging.*) I *asked* if I could help. Remember? You said no, no one could help. Remember?

SAM. (*Mocking.*) Sure, sure, Edgar.

EDGAR. (*Awe and disgust.*) My God, Sam; you don't *want* any help.

SAM. Well, not from you, Edgar; not from you.

EDGAR. (*Rises abruptly, moves to the window seat for his coat.*) Come on, Lu.

LUCINDA. (*Still with her broken crockery.*) But, Edgar, I'm just . . .

EDGAR. COME *ON!* If you think I'm going to stay and go through this!

CAROL. You two going? Did we hit an iceberg?

EDGAR. (*Quivering with rage.*) You staying? You wanna watch? O.K. You stay!

CAROL. (*Shrugs.*) G'by, rats.

LUCINDA. Don't you talk to Edgar that way!

CAROL. (*Moves away from them.*) I was talking to *both* of you.

EDGAR. (*To Sam.*) We came over here to *forgive* you!

SAM. (*Shakes his head; gently.*) It doesn't matter, Edgar.

EDGAR. (*Quivering with rage.*) How *dare* you let this happen to you!

LUCINDA. (*Realizing it.*) That's right! We came to forgive you!

SAM. (*To stop the exchange.*) It's all right; it doesn't matter.

EDGAR. How *dare* you let this happen! I'm not *here* anymore, Sam.

LUCINDA. (*Suddenly in tears.*) I never want to come here again! I never want to come to this house again! (*She runs out.*)

EDGAR. I'm not *here* anymore, Sam.

63

SAM. (*Pause; accepting.*) O.K., Edgar.

EDGAR. (*Sudden contained emotion.*) I'm not here, God damn you! (*Edgar backs into the hall, turns, exits.*)

CAROL. Three down and only me to go.

ELIZABETH. Aren't you bright! Why are you marrying that awful man?

CAROL. It's the *least* I can do.

ELIZABETH. You don't have to.

CAROL. I don't? Why don't I? He's on his way downhill; he's a barrel of laughs; he's a lush; he's a great fuck; I'm not doing anything else this week; I'm not twenty-two anymore, and I'm scared? Take your choice; they're all true.

ELIZABETH. (*This and the following both to the audience and generally to Sam and Carol.*) In the outskirts of Dubuque, on the farm, when I was growing up—back there, back then—I learned, with all the pigs and chickens and the endless sameness everywhere you looked, or thought, back there I learned—though I doubt I knew I was learning it—that all of the values were relative save one . . . "Who am I?" All the rest is semantics—liberty, dignity, possession. (*She leans forward; only to Sam now.*) There's only one that matters: "Who *am* I?"

SAM. (*Simple.*) I don't *know* who I am.

ELIZABETH. Then how can you possibly know who I am? (*Oscar appears on the balcony, dressed in Sam's nightshirt, nothing else. He poses.*)

OSCAR. (*To the group.*) Do I look well? Does it suit me? (*Carol giggles.*)

ELIZABETH. (*Claps her hands together in delight.*) Oscar! You are a dream!

JO. (*Looks up.*) Sam? Is that you?

SAM. (*Pain.*) Oh, Jo! Don't!

OSCAR. (*To Carol.*) Don't you think I make a splendid Sam?

JO. Sam? Is that you?

SAM. Jo? Please don't?

OSCAR. (*Arms wide; beatific.*) Am I not . . . am I, indeed, not Sam? (*To the audience.*) Am I not Sam?

CAROL. I'm going to untie him.

OSCAR. It's on your shoulders, pretty lady; you open the package, you take the present.

CAROL. That's O.K. by me; I'm not a friend. (*She unties Sam.*) Who the fuck tied these knots?

64

OSCAR. Duh menfolk; dey tied him up; dem's duh ones.

SAM. Jo?

JO. Sam?

CAROL. You *wanna* be untied, don't you?

SAM. Sure.

CAROL. It's the least I can do.

SAM. Don't go.

CAROL. Everyone else has gone.

SAM. Yes!

CAROL. (*Shrugs.*) What do you want me to do?

SAM. (*Lost little boy.*) Make Jo better? Make them go away? (*Oscar shakes his head; Elizabeth laughs gently.*)

CAROL. (*To Sam; gentle.*) Jo thinks she's better. They make her think so.

SAM. (*Chilling knowledge.*) Is that what matters?

CAROL. Ask Jo.

SAM. (*One final time; but soft, lost.*) Please? That's not Jo's mother?

CAROL. (*After a long pause; totally noncommittal.*) Right. I mean . . . who's to say? (*To the audience.*) Who's to say?

ELIZABETH. (*Rises, moves toward Carol.*) You're a very special lady.

CAROL. (*A rueful laugh.*) You're pretty special yourself. (*Looks up at Oscar; ironic.*) You're not so bad, either. (*She looks once more at Sam; exits.*)

OSCAR. (*Waves.*) Bye-bye; bye-bye.

SAM. (*Soft.*) Don't go.

JO. (*An echo.*) Bye-bye; bye-bye. (*A silence. Finally, Sam rushes from his chair, over to Jo. Elizabeth gestures Oscar not to interrupt. Sam kneels by Jo, grabs her by the shoulders, shakes her. We see that she is rubber. Oscar watches from his position on the stairs. Elizabeth stays where she was standing with Carol.*)

SAM. (*Tears; choking; loss; fury; tenderness.*) Do you want this? Hunh? (*Shakes her.*) Is this what you want!? Yes!?

ELIZABETH. (*Level; gentle.*) Of course she wants it. Just . . . let her go.

SAM. (*Shakes her.*) Because if this is what you want, I'm not any part of it; you've locked me out. I . . . I don't exist. I . . . I don't exist. Just . . . just *tell* me. (*Jo manages to look at him, puts her hands to his face, cups it.*)

JO. (*Explaining; gently.*) Please . . . just let me die? (*Sam pulls away, stares at her, wracked with sobs. To the audience; explaining.*) Just

let me die . . . please? (*Here her explanation begins to become pain.*)
PLEASE? . . . (*This time the word is prolonged as long as possible; it is urged out by pain; it is filled with gasps; to no one, to everyone. Now she grasps her belly in short spasms of pain.*) Anhhh! Anhhh! ANHHHHH! (*Oscar comes down the stairs to her.*)

OSCAR. All right; all right, now. (*Sam watches the following without moving from his position; his sobs continue, though.*)

JO. Aaaaaaaaaaaannnnnnnhhhh! Sweet Jesus! Aaaaaaaaaaannnnn-nnhhhhhhhh!

OSCAR. (*Scooping her into his arms.*) Let me help you.

SAM. Jo!

JO. (*Through her gasps; to Oscar.*) Just . . . get . . . me . . . up . . . stairs.

SAM. Jo?

OSCAR. (*As he carries her upstairs; soothing, crooning.*) I'll take care of you now; I'll make you better; you'll see; I'll put you right to bed; I'll make you better . . .

JO. Just get me . . . AAAANNNNHHHHHHH!

OSCAR. (*As he carries her Offstage.*) Shhhh, shhhh, shhhh; easy, now; easy. (*A howl from Offstage; another.*)

ELIZABETH. (*Moves to a chair; gently.*) She's dying, you see.

SAM. (*Sobs under; shivering.*) I'm dying.

ELIZABETH. Oh, no; not yet. You don't know what it *is*. (*A softer howl from upstairs; Elizabeth laughs abruptly; then smiles.*) I had a dream once about dying. Shall I tell it to you?

SAM. (*Shivering.*) No.

ELIZABETH. All right: I dreamt I was on a beach at sunset—with friends; we had a driftwood fire, I believe.

SAM. I don't want to know.

ELIZABETH. (*Begins to share this with the audience, too.*) There were seagulls in the distance, and there was the sound of the surf—but muted, for it was sunset.

SAM. I don't want to know.

ELIZABETH. And all at once . . . it became incredibly quiet; the waves stopped, and the gulls hung there in the air.

SAM. No? Please?

ELIZABETH. Such silence. And then it began; the eastern horizon was lighted by an explosion, hundreds of miles away—no sound! And then another, to the west—no sound! And within seconds they were everywhere, always at a great distance—the flash of light, and silence.

SAM. Please?

ELIZABETH. We knew what we were watching, and there was no time to be afraid. The silence was . . . beautiful as the silent bombs went off. Perhaps we were already dead; perhaps that was why there was no sound. (*A silence.*)

SAM. (*A shivering little boy.*) That was . . . that was the end of the world.

ELIZABETH. (*A pause; comforting; to Sam, now.*) I though that's what we were talking about. (*To the audience.*) Isn't that what we were talking about? (*Oscar appears in the upstairs hallway, dressed in his own clothes. To Oscar.*) Is it all right?

OSCAR. (*Looks down at them.*) Yes; it's all right. (*Indicates.*) And that one?

ELIZABETH. He's better; calmer.

SAM. (*Still the little boy.*) It *is* true, isn't it? What you told me?

ELIZABETH. (*Dreamy.*) No sound? No time to be afraid? Everything done before you know it?

SAM. Yes. It is true?

ELIZABETH. Everything is true.

OSCAR. (*Descending. Quietly; to Elizabeth; to Sam.*) Therefore, nothing is true.

ELIZABETH. (*Looks up at him.*) Therefore, everything is true. (*She smiles.*)

OSCAR. (*Descending. He smiles; an endearment.*) Oh, Elizabeth. (*A silence.*)

SAM. And Jo?

ELIZABETH. (*Tiny pause.*) Don't worry about Jo.

OSCAR. We can go now.

ELIZABETH. (*Vaguely, momentarily surprised.*) What? Yes, of course we can. (*She stands.*)

SAM. No time to be afraid?

ELIZABETH. No! No time!

SAM. (*More insistent.*) No time to be afraid!?

ELIZABETH. No! No time! Everything done before you know it.

SAM. . . . Before I know it.

ELIZABETH. Everything done.

OSCAR. (*Faintly contemptuous, to the audience.*) Nothing is retained; nothing. Come.

ELIZABETH. All right.

SAM. (*Finally; timid; to Elizabeth.*) Who are you? Really?

ELIZABETH. (*Looks at him for a moment.*) Why, I'm the lady from Dubuque. I thought you knew. (*To the audience.*) I thought he knew.

CURTAIN

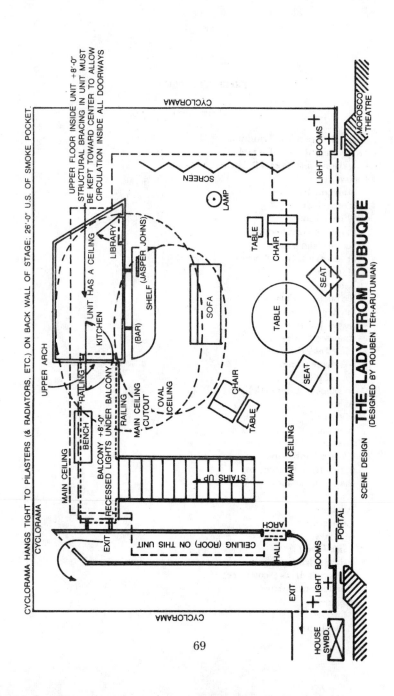

THE LADY FROM DUBUQUE

(DESIGNED BY ROUBEN TER-ARUTUNIAN)

SCENE DESIGN

69

PROPERTY PLOT

Preset—Act I

Move: R. chair to Act I position
Set: pillow D.R. of coffee table
Check: water and Kleenex R. kitchen, bedroom
On Bar:
  Bourbon decanter
  Scotch decanter
  Wine decanter
  Empty spritzer bottle
  Six (6) clean glasses
  Fred's drink (Scotch, ice)
  Matches
  Ashtray
  Ice bucket with ice
  Pitcher with water
  Jasper Johns
  Assorted bottles
On Side Table R.:
  Jo's drink (wine)
  Vial of pills
  Jo's shoes (under table)
  Ashtray
On Ottoman:
  Ashtray
On Coffee Table:
  Carol's drink (wine)
  Sam's drink (Scotch, ice)
  Platter of canapés
  Two (2) ashtrays
  Art book
  Cigarettes
  Matches
On Side Table L.:
  Edgar's drink (ice *only*)
  Lucinda's drink (Scotch, ice)
  Canapé on napkin
  Cigarettes
  Matches
  Telephone

Kitchen:
Two (2) full spritzer bottles
Coffee service (2 trays)
Check:
Both doors *closed*
L. *masking* in place
Carol's blouse on bench
Lucinda's purse on bench
Carol's purse on coffee table (cigs. in purse)

Preset—Act II

Move:
R. chair to upstage marks
Strike:
All party glasses, napkins, cig. butts.
Jo's shoes, Jo's pills
Bar:
Check clean glass for Fred
Enough Scotch for one drink
Clear space for coffee tray
Sofa:
Elizabeth's coat, hat, gloves, purse L. end of sofa
Broken cup on carpet U. of R. end of sofa
Kitchen:
Recheck both coffee trays
Both doors closed
Work light out
Bench:
Oscar's coat and hat
Replace:
L. masking
Furniture:
Sofa, 2 arm-less chairs—all in black leather, Bauhaus style
2 poufs, same style as above
1 bench, same style as above
1 glass vase with dogwood branches, arranged in it
Grey screen, oversize
Glass-top coffee table, 4′6″ diam.
Plexi-glass bar/shelf attached to *US* unit
Jaspar Johns "6" hanging above shelf at left end

COSTUME PLOT

ACT I

Jo

    Pale turquoise silk over blouse with mandarin collar, mid-thigh length
    Deep blue pajama trousers
    Turquoise slippers (never worn, preset on stage)

Sam

    Designer blue jeans
    Beige and brown striped silk shirt
    Camel cashmere V-neck sweater
    Brown Gucci loafers
    Brown belt

Edgar

    Dark brown wool trousers
    Forest green shawl collar sweater
    Green, brown and beige striped shirt
    cordovan belt and loafers

Lucinda

    Peach crepe dress with ecru lace collar
    Beige purse and pumps
    Double strand of pearls
    Engagement ring and wedding band

Fred

    Brown, corduroy
    Brown, blue and beige plaid shirt
    Brown suede shoes

Carol

    Violet pleated trousers
    Magenta glitter sweater
    Lavender high heel sandals
    Lavender clutch bag
    Striped violet and magenta organdy shirt (carried, not worn)

Elizabeth

    Bright red wool coat
    Blue grey dyed fox boa
    Deep blue grey hat, gloves, purse, shoes, dress
    Single strand large pearls
    3 large golden rings

Oscar

>Brown/violet 3 piece suit
>Pink shirt with white collar
>Olive green and red striped tie
>Brown shoes
>Black Chesterfield coat
>Black bowler hat
>Black leather gloves
>White silk scarf

Act II

Jo

>Nightgown with lace and embroidery
>Pale orchid handkerchief cotton

Sam

>Striped nightshirt/brown leather slippers
>(same jeans as Act I)
>Pale blue Oxford cloth shirt
>(underdress stomach protection for punch)
>Brown loafers and belt

Edgar

>Pale grey herringbone sportcoat
>Grey flannel trousers
>Pale blue Oxford cloth shirts
>Deep rust sleeveless V/neck sweater
>Cordovan belt and loafers

Lucinda

>Beige silk blouse
>Beige gabardine skirt
>Brown on brown striped silk jacket
>Gold metallic chain belt
>Beige pumps and purse

Fred

>Camel wool blazer
>Tan trousers
>Red and beige plaid shirt
>Brown suede shoes
>Brown belt (heavy duty-ties Sam's hands with it)

Carol

>Pale blue fitted pullover sweater
>Taupe wool skirt with slit
>Black sling-back shoes
>Black clutch bag

Elizabeth
   Same as Act I without coat, hat, gloves, scarf
Oscar
   Same as Act I remove coat, hat, gloves, scarf
   Duplicate Sam nightshirt, slippers